Handle Ur Biz

Chronicles of A Hustler 1

By Tarik Adams

Disclaimer

This book is fictional and designed for entertainment purposes only. The content contained within each chapter is the sole expression, creative thought process, and opinion of its author. Names, Characters, Places, and incidents are the products of the author's imagination or are used fictionally. Any resemblance to actual events, locates, or persons, living or dead, is entirely coincidental.

Dedications

I dedicate this to God and above all, my mother who has always had my back. Also to my Aunt Fay that stuck through my whole bid with me.

Acknowledgements

My family, my cousins: Tia, Ciara, Gabe, and the few friends I do have...you know who you are I thank you for your love. To my homegirl, Celena, for writing to me through my whole bid, and for making my time go by easier with every letter you wrote. To my main man, Paulie V. who also made my bid easier with endless nights of laughing and the encouragement to keep writing. And to all of my Gs locked up doing time in the belly of the beast...this is for you. Keep your Head Up!

A lot of the things that happen in this book are things that really happened in my life and some of the events that happen are embellished a little to make the book a little more interesting for my readers. You be the judge of what's true and what's not. It's a book...let your mind go.

~Tarik Adams, aka, Mr. Handle Ur Biz

Introduction To a Hustler

People say the apple doesn't fall far from the tree. I guess that's true with me and my pops; even though I've only met him twice in my life, once at the age of seven, and again at twenty-two, we had a lot in common. What we had in common was in my bloodline; from the start pimpin' and dealing drugs.

Well, before I get into all of this, let me introduce myself; they call me Mr. Handle Ur Biz, which I'll get into how I got that name much later in the story. It's gonna be a long ride and I'll go back and forth through my years of life. Right now, I'm thirty-five at the time of writing this in jail. Yup…in jail. I only have five months left in my one-year bid and decided to start a book.

I've done a lot in my thirty-five years of life including selling my first couple of ounces of weed in seventh grade at the age of thirteen. But I had been around drugs my entire childhood. My mom and aunt were crackheads and my uncle was a pimp. They say that when you are in the hood, there are no doctors and lawyers to look up to. I guess that's the case with me. I'm going to jump forward to my life at sixteen years old and I'll come back to my childhood later.

At a young age, I was already pimpin'. I was just too square of a dude to realize it. My first hoe was named Courtney. I could get this girl to do anything. I didn't know the power I had inside of me. She was a young white girl who was not bad on the eyes, but not a ten by a long shot. She came from a rich family, had her own car, and two years of life on me. At first I just got money and rides from her, that's where it started seeing that she had a couple of years on me. She had a serious head game, as in, she could suck good dick. That bitch could make a nigga cum in minutes. At first her and her girl would come down and give me and my boy, D-Man head in the car.

My boy was always like, "Damn, man. I wish my chick sucked dick like that. Your chick gives animal top; my chick ain't doing shit back here. I wanna try that."

I told him, "Give me fifty dollars, buy me a forty ounce, and I'll see what I can do."

Well, you already know I made that shit happen. I always had an ill mouth game, so I told the hoe that if she cared about me that she would have to prove it. She didn't know about the deal I had already made; I can't remember what I spent the fifty dollars on, but I drank that forty ounce before I could even tap into it.

D-Man came out the room like, "Damn, I couldn't even hold it in!"

She made him cum in like fifty-six seconds. I laughed to myself knowing I had something good with that girl. She only lasted a couple of years, but she wouldn't be the last to bring a young nigga that paper. Courtney eventually moved to D.C. for college, but she paid for visits for me and my cousin to come see her and she sent me money for a while, but my game was young.

I let so many girls go in my youth. They meant nothing to me. I had no love for these hoes; just the dough. I was always close to my mom, but she knew the game. Damn, she was with my pops, so she never gave me problems when she saw them come and go.

My pops gave me two things from his bloodline: game and a set of eyes that a bitch would die for. Like I said, I only met him twice: once when I was seven, my mom and I flew to Barbados to meet him. We stayed for a couple of weeks and came back to Boston. My mom always told me that he never had a green card and that he got deported and couldn't come back. I knew that was only half the truth. He can't come back, but not because of the green card. While he was in America, which was only for five years, he stacked a million dollars. Back in the early '80s a million was about five million in today's currency, but after stacking the money, things hit the fan.

He pushed mad weight and started a cab company which was a front for his pimpin'. He had five cabs moving all over New England with eight of the baddest bitches walking. This is how it worked, you would call a cab like you normally do, but the chick behind the wheel wasn't a cab driver. She would bring you to a hotel, help you in with your bags and you can figure out the rest.

Everything was good until a new bitch wasn't feeling the love. When she got caught up with five kilos in the back of a car while speeding back from New York, backed into a corner by the Feds, she gave up everything on the operation. But that didn't stop my pops. His money was long. He got locked up and was able to bail out quickly. Well, needless to say, that bitch came up missing. But while on bail, the Feds were on to my pops and his love for that paper and the game. They knew he wouldn't stop, and he didn't.

It took the Feds a year before they caught up with pops again. This time a punk ass pimp named Sunshine started to notice his pockets were getting low and saw that a couple of his bottom bitches (main girls) chose my pops. He knew just where to look for them. He caught one of his old bitches at a club one night and beat the breaks off that bitch. When she got a hold of my pops he saw her face and went crazy. Having that island blood in him, he snapped like four Jamaican dreads and rolled out that same night looking for Sunshine. My pops found the pimp at his strip club called, Afterdark. I'm not sure what was up with that dude going by the name of Sunshine and having a nightclub called Afterdark, but I guess that is how he liked to roll back then.

Pops and his underboss waited outside and when Sunshine came out, the tech rang shot after shot with Sunshine catching two to the head. But not before his bodyguard lit the Benz up with a couple of their own, killing my pop's soldier. When the Benz drove off, the tires were blown, so he didn't make it far before he was surrounded by half of Boston PD. He wiped his prints off of the gun and placed it in his already dead boy's hand. Having a good lawyer and claiming his innocence, my pops was deported back to Barbados, never to leave the island again.

Having stacked mad dough, he was even more of a kingpin on the island once he returned. Even though the island is only 21 miles from top to bottom, life wasn't over for him having been sent back there as a punishment. The way in which he returned, just made him a legend there. So when I went with my mom to visit him when I was seven, he was more powerful than ever. I didn't find out until I went to find him when I was twenty-two, that he had asked my mom to marry him while we were there the first time.

When I asked her why she didn't marry him, she said, "He was too deep in the game and I was afraid that we both might be kidnapped someday for a ransom, sooner or later."

While back on the island, my pops money stacked to over ten million and he had shipments of the rawest coke shipped in and shipped back out. After cutting, the load was doubled up and he shipped north, south, east and west of the island using Barbados as the center point of his organization. He had soldiers that would kill for him walking around with techs and machine guns at his every move.

My mother also told me that some of the other things she saw on the island when we visited that bothered and put fear in her was the fact that he was treated like a god everywhere he went. The night life was crazy and she told me that the soldiers would lick off rounds of ammo before and after they left. To go anywhere, six cars followed his Benz with anywhere from ten to fifteen soldiers loading all the cars. I once recalled going back to the hotel we were staying in that I went into a suitcase of his and saw so much money that I thought I was in a movie.

As I went to close the suitcase, he walked in and asked, "What do you think you are doing?"

I was shook; nothing came out of my mouth at first. After a few seconds, I finally stirred up a couple of words and asked, "Where did you get all of this."

I'll never forget what he said.

"Sometimes you got to do dirt to get what you want."

After he said that, he snatched the suitcase and put it on a shelf that I could not reach. I knew right then and there that I would do whatever it took to get a suitcase full of money for myself.

Chapter 1

After a couple of weeks, my mom and I flew back to the states and I didn't see or hear from my pops for another fifteen years. I had so many dreams about that suitcase over the next couple of years. In each dream, I saw him standing over me saying, *Handle Ur Biz, son.* By the time I was ten, I was making little moves here and there.

I first started out as a look-out for a small gang selling drugs in the projects of Malden, Mass. Newland Street Projects had a gang called P.O.D. – Posse Of Destruction. At that time, 1988, crack was everywhere and these dudes had three crack houses and I would skip school and be a look-out for ten bucks a day. That was a lot for a poor black kid; sometimes I'd end up with a hundred dollars a week and I didn't spend shit. I didn't care about Jordans and shit like that at the time, I didn't even buy a pair until I was sitting on my first couple of stacks.

At that point, I was eleven with $3,000 saved. I had more dough than most of the Gs that were running around selling the shit, but it didn't last long because I turned from a boy to a man and my view changed a lil. I started to notice how my uncle and the older pimps did their thing, plus I started to notice females in a whole different way...which reminds me of the second chick that chose me.

I was seventeen and she was twenty-four. Her name was Crystal and she was a dime piece. She looked like the singer, Pink, but with bigger tits. She was a stripper. Although she never sold her pussy for me, who knows what the hoe did to get that paper. All I know that she bought me my first car and taught me how to drive a standard. She came through my life about a year or so after Courtney. She was making bank at the strip club and would buy me anything I wanted.

My first car was a BMW 325 that Crystal paid for. I didn't complain, we fucked on and off for the next couple of years. She had a condo on exit one in Nashua, NH; right over the Mass boarder. I stayed at her crib while she was at work. She would always leave me an ounce of that loud and a bottle of Henny. When Crystal would come home, I was so drunk and high, I would blow her back out for a couple of hours and that's what kept her in love with me; or at least I think that's why she loved me the way that she did. I was young with mad energy; and boy…did she have a wet pussy at that point. It was a win-win situation for both of us.

Although I was banging three or four other chicks at the time, especially with my new ride which sat on chrome 19's, with a black paint job, glitter in it that would sparkle when the sun hit it and a flip out TV with a PS2 in it. My ride seemed to turn bitches' heads left and right, and I still was putting it down on Crystal every chance I got and any time she wanted it. I was doing my thing; all while still in high school. At that point, I slowed down with the drug game. I'd make a move here and there, but I was more worried about school.

Going back to the $3,000 I had saved when I was eleven, that didn't last long. I blew at least $2,000 on gear, trying to look like a young pimp. My mom started to notice the clothes and one day, I came back from the block and she was there with a look on her face and a letter in her hand. Even though she got high, she always worked a lot, that's how I was able to skip so much school. On that particular day, she came home early and had gotten to the mail before me. In it was a letter from the school saying that I had missed 92 days of school. She lit my lil ass up! She didn't care how I got the clothes, but she always stressed to me the importance of getting a good education.

I respected my mom. She had me at a young age – nineteen, and she always held it down with a roof over my head, so after that beating, I took my black ass back to school for the next couple of years and stayed off the streets. But by the time I reached thirteen, I couldn't be broke any longer and had to cop a lil sumthin' to stay afloat.

I was thirteen now, and I grabbed two ounces of weed for $160, bagged it up in all dime bags, and made $560 in two days; $400 in profit. I went on that way grabbing a couple of zips here and there just to keep my gear tight and to have a couple hundred in my pocket. The next couple of years were school, hoes, and a couple of flips. By the time I meet Crystal, I was about to be a senior in high school and her wanting to spend more and more time with a young G was just too much. I had to handle my biz and she needed more time than I could give her, so I pushed her away. I was young and dumb; she was a gold mine. I looked at it like, *I'm young and I don't need a bitch stressing me out.* She blew up my pager so much over the next couple of months, that I had my older girl cousin go smack the shit out of her. My cousin, Tia, is a straight female G. Pretty ass face, but built like a short linebacker. Crystal wouldn't be the last chick that Tia would smack for me.

Tia was also the first one to fully explain the crack game to me. She would drive me around in her gold Lexus 300. She also would school me on everything I needed to know about the game; from how to get a fiend /crack head on the line, what to look out for, how to cook it, weight it, and everything else about the game. I wish I had followed all of her advice, because if I would have listened, it would have saved me from catching my first case.

She always said, "Don't base on a crackhead."

I wish I would have remembered that at age twenty-two. But I'm getting a little ahead of myself.

So, now I'm seventeen; my pimp game is starting, and my couple of flips of weed – mixed with a couple of sales of crack – had my pockets straight and yet, I don't even have my diploma. I'm pulling up in a hooked up Beamer on the regular and the bitches were on me. My cousin, Tia, got me a fake ID, so I was already clubbing and hitting the bars and strip clubs – going through hoes like underwear. I had no clue that love was right around the corner; which as you should know, has no space in a young pimp's life. You can't love these hoes; M.O.B. (Money Over Bitches)

Chapter 2

Well, there were two things I fell in love with; the first was stickups, which right off the bat had me like a crackhead junkie. I achieved that love going into my senior year when I was introduced to it by my cousin, Galen – who if he had not blown out his knee six months earlier, would have gone pro his freshman year he played varsity everything from baseball, football to basketball. But his knee went out because a fat lineman fell on it, and so did his hopes of a football career. From then on, he turned into a straight beast; which wasn't hard for him given his background playing sports.

From the time that we were kids, Galen and I were bigger than most of the other kids. At the time he weighed in at six feet tall and over 230 pounds of pure muscle. We were close since he was my first cousin. Our mothers were sisters and we were only one week apart in age. He was born on January 31, 1978 and I was born one week later on February 7, 1978 during the blizzard. We were more than cousins; we were closer than blood.

Because of our closeness, when he called me for our first stickup, there was no doubt in my mind that I was down. The fact that he had a team of gorillas to go along with him that, made my decision even easier. Besides me on his team, Galen had three others.

Damond was one of the smallest at 5'8" and 175 pounds; but he was as strong as an ox. Later in life, I saw him carry a 300 pound safe about 100 yards to load it into the back of a truck. Now that's some muscle to have as one of your soldiers. Secondly, there was a white boy named Randy. He was an animal; all juiced out, 6'3" and about 250 pounds of all muscle. Lastly, there was a brother we called Train, and he had that name for a good reason. He could run through anything and kick any door off the frame. He was also about 6'3" and 260 pounds. Add me and my 5'10", 205 frame to the mix with Galen and his friends, and we had an all-star lineup.

I did not know the dude that we were about to get, but my cousin had already scooped it out. The dude was a drug dealer/rapper from Lowell, Mass. They called him KK. I had to give it to the dude…he had it going on at twenty years old. He had two Benzes, a 300 and a 500. He also had a couple of motorcycles and owned a three-family house that he had set up like the Carter in *New Jack City*. The third floor was where he bagged and cut his drugs. He had a system set up like those deposit machines at the ATM drive-thru where he had a tube that ran through all three floors and you would put the order in and he would send the money up from the first floor. Whatever you ordered would then be shot back down from the top floor. The second floor was $10,000 studio with a lounge to chill in, a pool table, jacuzzi, a bar and a lot of other fly shit. The first floor was set up like an apartment.

All five of us drove around Lowell for a couple of hours before we were supposed to go in. My cousin was smooth; he would wait till about 3:00 or 4:00 am before going into any house.

He made sure everyone was asleep; especially the next door neighbors and people across the street so that no one would ever see what was going on. If they heard a loud bang, we were already in the house by the time they got up to look out the window.

The house had back steps that went all the way up all three flights and had back doors to all of them. Train was to go through the first floor front door. Damond was supposed to go through the back door on the first floor; Randy through the second floor back door, and me and my cousin Galen were supposed to take the third floor back door.

We all got into place with Train being the last one in so he could not be seen by anyone sitting on their front porch. We all had our watches set to the same time; right down to the second. At 4:00 am, we kicked all the doors in at the same time. My cuz kicked the door and I followed. There were two big ass dudes sitting at the table with shot guns by their feet. All you could smell was weed in the air; I think that's why they were so slow to react. By the time the first dude reached for his gun, my cousin had already smacked him with the nine above his left eye. It sounded like a big branch snapping. By the time the second dude looked up, I was all over him telling him, "Don't even think about it or you will have two put in you." I think he was so high that all he could do was laugh.

I put one in his kneecap with a .22. He fell to the floor; blood started to pour everywhere and my cousin ordered the other dude to duct tape him once he stopped bitching about the lump above his eye. I duct tapped him when he was done while my cousin loaded all the drugs and money into a duffle bag. Train went through the first floor door. You could hear the door kicked in all the way upstairs. Then Damond and Randy came in at the same time. When Train entered the house there was nobody around. He scanned the first two rooms to find KK in bed with two Asian chicks, butt naked. They were duct tapped quickly. Damond entered the back door through the kitchen and found two fly ass Spanish chicks cooking. They also got duct tapped.

Randy went through the second floor back door where he found two young niggas using the studio. Randy is a big boy, and the dudes were so shaken when he came in the door that one of them pissed on himself. I hope that dude wasn't trying to be a gangster rapper because he would have to change his name to Pee Wee Herman after that incident. The dudes were duct tapped also; I doubt if that was even needed given the fact that they were both only fifteen or sixteen, so they posed no threat to us or Randy.

Randy grabbed a pound or two that was lying on a table, while Train and Damond searched the crib and found a safe in the bedroom closet. It was bolted to the floor. They used a crowbar to pry it loose. Damond snatched it up. It weighed about 300 pounds. Within minutes, we were all running toward the Tahoe about a hundred yards away. It was our first lick together as a team and we all walked away with about $50,000 apiece. There was about $100,000 in the safe and fifty pounds of weed upstairs, four keys and like $20,000.

We – meaning all of us except my cousin because he didn't smoke – split the two pounds of weed Randy found on the second floor. A half a pound for the head, plus $50,000 wasn't bad, and remember, I was only seventeen at the time; I was happy as shit even though I had to shoot someone. To this day, I wonder if dude walked with a limp.

The second vic went even easier than the first. This fat ass dude, Corey…this nigga was big; about 6'6" and 400 pounds; all of it sloppy. He was pushing major weight from what we heard. He was always talking about, "I wish a nigga would…" Well, we were about to find out if his word was bond.

This time though, only three of us went. Train and Randy played for a college in Upstate NY; Albany. They had a football game and couldn't go; so it was just me, Damond and my cousin Galen. This dude, Corey, lived with his girl and a young kid, so we were sure we didn't need any other help. It took us two visits to get the job done. The first night we went and just sat outside the place till almost 5:00 am. Corey was still awake with his fat ass, watching ESPN, but it wasn't the fact that he was up that stopped us from going in. His next door neighbors were up all night. I think they were having a card game or something, because they had a lot of company. I was heated because I wanted that shit to happen. I didn't like the dude Corey. He was a pussy and was always talking about gangster shit because he had done a year or two Upstate. But I knew he was a pussy. Even though he was a couple of years older than I was, he still would hang out at high school parties. I've seen him called out tons of times. I was about to see how much Kool-Aid his heart pumped.

The next night, we were back at his place around 2:00 am. My cousin and I sat in the woods behind his house where we could see into it through one of those sliding glass doors. Damond was parked out front just in case Corey's bitch ass made a run for it. We waited until 3:30 am; all of the lights on the street were out and he turned off the TV and walked up a flight of stairs. We were in all black, masked up, with our vests on. I had a .22 and my cuz loved his 9mm. He also had a duffle bag over his back, duct tape and a crowbar like always.

Fifteen minutes after our vic went upstairs, it was on. My cousin rushed up the back porch and with one swift kick, the glass sliding door fell down. I was surprised the glass didn't break, but damn…it made a loud bang when it hit the ground. Corey must have not been asleep yet because he appeared at the top of the stairs, rubbing his eyes STD (scared to death). He was frozen like a deer in headlights; such a shame for all four hundred pounds of his fat ass. My cousin was up the flight of stairs so quickly. He took the stairs three at a time with his nine already banging off the right side of his head. My cousin loved to pistol whip niggas. Corey's fat ass fell to his knees and started crying. I guess that gangster walk was all talk like I knew it was.

Bang. The gun hit Corey again in his head. He made a wrong move and tried to grab the gun. He shouldn't have done that because my cousin came crashing down with three more blows to the side of his head. His shit began to swell real quickly. He looked like Arturo Gatti after a fight. Corey wouldn't stop crying; his girl was at the bedroom door, and we made her duct tape him. She was calmer than his bitch ass. She then opened up the safe. There were stacks of money inside, but no work. We told him that if he didn't tell us where the work was at, we were going to go up side his head some more. He was still crying like a newborn. He only stopped for a second when his girl told us that it was in the kitchen in the cereal boxes. He cut her a look that would kill, but even she knew he was a pussy at this point. She looked back at him like...*I know you don't want these niggas to hit your bitch ass again.*

I went downstairs while my cousin made the girl duct tape her own feet, and then he did her hands. There were five boxes of cereal in the cabinet; two filled with coke and ecstasy. By the time I put it in the duffle bag, my cousin was back down the stairs. It took us about seven or eight minutes for the whole stickup and we had made a quick $150,000; $50,000 apiece. Again...this meant more for me... because I didn't like that nigga, I gave my cousin and Damond $5,000 apiece extra. So I walked away with $40,000. I was on top of the world. It was five months before I would even graduate high school and I had about $120,000 in my stash.

Over the next two months, we would have a couple of more licks. We had the whole team back for the third one, so it went real smooth. But with five heads in on it, the take was light; only $15,000 apiece. I was cool though. Shit...I was sitting on almost $150,000.

The fourth hit didn't go so well and it would be a huge eye opener to me. See, I wasn't built like these niggas. Shit...I was a G and all, but these fools were crazy and I was about to find out just how crazy they really were. They all played football; I played a little Pop Warner. These dudes loved to hurt motherfuckers and didn't care about getting hurt. Shit...every house we had been in, my cousin found some way to go up side someone's head. I shot a nigga, but I still have dreams about that shit all the time. I wasn't a killer and I knew this.

This fourth vic was supposed to be our biggest hit yet. Then we were all going to chill for the summer. My cousin was fucking a girl that was bartending for a card game that these Italian dudes had twice a month. She thought the guys might be connected, but we didn't care. There was about a million thrown on the table at any given game, so that was enough for us. She gave us the whole layout. The house was huge; it was on a dirt road in Andover, Mass, with the nearest neighbor about a half a mile away. So we didn't have to worry about being seen. There were going to be about five cars in the driveway with the drivers strapped. Next to the driveway, was a door that lead into the kitchen were all the wives would be cooking and a total of six or seven other women there that were maids who served the food. The rest of the house was empty.

When we got into the house, I couldn't believe how big the shit was. It was definitely a mansion. It looked like the house the Jamaican dude, Ox, had in the movie, *Belly*. We dropped Randy, Damond and Train off on the back side where they would have to walk a mile or so through the woods to sneak up behind the drivers. Galen and I were simply going to drive up the driveway; once the drivers saw the headlights, they would be alert, but it would give the rest of the team time to sneak up behind them.

It was about 11:45 pm by the time the team was set and ready for action. We drove up the driveway slow. We could see the five drivers noticing the car. At first, they were standing outside of their cars, reading newspapers, drinking coffee, talking and bullshitting. Once they noticed the Tahoe creeping up the driveway, they quickly reached for their guns; all standing with their backs to the woods. We stopped the truck halfway up the driveway and shut off the lights. By the time the lights flicked back on, the boys were ready. A shotgun in Damond's hands, randy had two nines, and Train had an AR-15 pointed to the back of the driver's heads. They dropped their guns and we jumped out of the truck and grabbed the guns while they were being tied up. By this point in our licks, we had ditched duct tape for those big plastic zip ties that the police sometimes use. They were quick and nearly impossible to get out of.

We placed the drivers back in the cars and entered the side door into the kitchen. All you could smell was food. Whatever they were cooking made a nigga hungry. Those women could cook their asses off and the wives were fly ass shit! All six of them could be on those *Housewives* reality shows or some shit like that. They were all in their thirties, but you couldn't tell. They were tan with dark hair, big boobs and dressed to kill. I'd would have wifed all of them up and I'm known for pulling some bad bitches. The wait staff was also in the kitchen and they were some dimes as well. They were in their twenties and all dressed in black, fitted cat suits. Whoever these dudes were who were playing cards, they had very good taste in women.

The ladies were caught off guard talking and preparing plates. They didn't even notice us standing there. When one of the wives turned and noticed us, she let out a scream. I placed my hand over her mouth and told the bitch to shut up or that would be the last scream she ever made. The house was so big we were sure that no one had heard her scream. All the women were tied up one by one.

One of the women kept saying, "Do you know who you are about to fuck with!"

By the second or third time she said it, Galen smacked the shit out of her and said, "Bitch, do you know who you are fucking with!"

He was dead serious. He had no fear. My cousin was crazy. Having a bad childhood and watching his dream of playing for the pros fade away turned him into a beast.

The card game was set up on the other side of the house. It felt like it took us ten minutes to get there. *Damn, this house was big!* Train was the first to enter and we followed. All you could smell was cigar smoke and cognac. Six fat Italian dudes sat around at a round table dressed like straight bosses; Dons in fact. They reminded me of John Gotti. There had to be at least a million dollars sitting on the table. The girl that my cousin was messing with was behind a bar directly behind the card table. At first they were all talking and one of them looked up and noticed us. The look on his face alerted the others to turn around.

My cousin spoke first and said, "This can all go easy and no one needs to get hurt. Your wives and drivers are safe."

One of the dudes interrupted and said, "Do you know who you are fucking with?"

Galen replied, "No! But people keep asking me that question like I give a fuck!"

Without any notice, one of the fat Dons reached for his ankle and everyone but me let their guns go. By the time the smoke cleared, all six men were lying in a pool of blood; even the girl was caught in the head. The man that reached for his ankle had a knife clinched in his hands. Damn, I don't know what he was thinking. You don't bring a knife to a gun fight. I was in shock. My ears were ringing. Finally, I snapped out of it when I heard my cousin yelling.

"Nigga, I said put the money in the bag. What's wrong with you!"

I didn't say anything. I started to place the cash in the bag. Train, Damond and Randy were taking Rolexes and Movados off the dead men and searching their pockets.

Galen went over to the dude with the knife in his hands and kicked him and said, "You stupid motherfucker, now we have to kill everyone because of you. If you just would have listened, you could have all been going home!"

I thought, *Damn, seven people dead and ten more ladies in the kitchen and the five drivers, that's like twenty-two people...all about to die.*

I didn't want any part of this, but it was too late for that shit. So, I didn't say anything, but I guess my cousin noticed the look on my face because he told me to take the bags to the truck and wait outside. While I was sitting in the truck, Randy and Train got the drivers out of the car and pulled them in the kitchen. All I could hear was the roars of the AR going off. It sounded like a war in that bitch!

*Blocka. Blocka. Blocka...*from the nines; and you could hear the shotgun bark a couple of times. Flashes of light came out of the windows. We left the mansion and headed to split up the money. There was $850,000 in cash and a couple of Rolexes, Breitling and

Movados. I didn't want a dead man's watch; it wasn't lucky for him, it wasn't going to be lucky for me. We split the money up with my cousin getting the most for setting it up. I got $150,000; that added with my stash meant that I was sitting on $300,000. It was time for me to lay back for a while or I might not see the age of eighteen. My cousin understood my thought process, seeing that he was just a week older than me, but he didn't stop doing his thing. He loved that shit.

Two days later, a maid found all twenty-two of the dead bodies. The newspaper read, *Five South Boston And Rhode Island Mafia Bosses Found Dead and Twelve Other Unidentified Bodies.* It also said that the deaths were the worst murders since the Valentine's Day Massacre. They assumed that another mafia family had done the killing.

They weren't that far off track; it was just another type of crime on crime. Only in this case, the perpetrators weren't the usual suspects as they say.

Chapter 3

By this time, I was turning eighteen and my cousin had just had a big bash for his eighteenth birthday. I didn't want a party; I had too much fun at his, and I was just going to chill on mine. Plus, I was planning mad trips for the summer. It was 1996 and I had family in California and Arizona and my boy D-Man had just moved to West Palm Beach in Florida. I was gonna stay a month at each and then come back and start college.

I went to California where my cousin, Ciara, lived. She and I were close in age too; she was ten days older than me. Her mom was white and her dad was black. She was pretty and smart at the same damn time. She looked like the singer Aaliyah. We got along well. It was my first time on the West Coast. She had been there since she was thirteen, but we kept in touch the whole time, so we didn't skip a beat. She knew how I got down; she didn't care. Her dad was a G, so she understood the life. Ciara was going to be a teacher and eventually a principal. She had goals and I knew she would achieve them. She was that type of person.

When I got there, we went everywhere. I had to see LA, Las Vegas; shit…I even wanted to see Compton and Crenshaw. Dr. Dre and Snoop was hot at that time; plus, *Boyz N the Hood* was a good ass flic.

My cousin said, "We can go, but only during the day cause those niggas are crazy."

I didn't complain though I had taken a plane and was on vacation, so I had left the burner at home.

I was spending money like crazy. I rented a 600 Benz for the month; $5,000 for the month wasn't bad. I shopped like a chick. Seeing that LA had hot fashion, I was on a Perry Ellis trip at the time and dropped another $5,000 in gear. I didn't even wear half the shit, but I was going to be on vacation for three months, so I wanted good shit. I wasn't much of a gambler, but I lost $15,000 in Vegas quick as shit too. I don't know what I was thinking.

While at a place called City Walk, where mad famous people hang out, we bumped into Brandy the singer and took pictures with her. She was big at the time and Ray J was with her, but that nigga was young; running around like a little kid and shit. Brandy was cool though; I'd hit that…at least back then I would.

We also met John Witherspoon. He was the dad in the movie, *Friday*. Now that man is funny and mad cool. He was with his family going into the movies. He just had a baby cause he had on one of those things that strap a baby to your chest. He broke his wife off with $100 and told her he was going to take a quick pic and to go inside and get the tickets. Now that's a star out with his family, but yet takes the time to take a quick picture with some kids…true star in my eyes. Plus, my cousin's boyfriend at the time, asked him to say something funny and he squeezed us into the picture and was like, "Come on, hurry up. Let's take this pic…you want me to say something funny…shit, I'm like sixty years old and just had a baby, I shouldn't be able to get it up!" *Snap*, the camera went off. He's a funny dude. Perfect timing.

What's also strange about seeing stars is that I didn't even notice them most of the time, but since my cousin had been out there so long, she could see a mile away and would just point them out. I had a blast while I was there and even told Ciara that I wanted to move out there. I dropped $30,000 in a month.

After that, I was off to Arizona. I took my cousin with me. She knew her way around there too; plus, she was going to college there. Now Arizona has some bad ass white chicks. I love white girls. But Arizona was different; there were so many dimes out there and they didn't even know they were dimes. Shit…in Boston and New York, those bitches they are bad and they have the attitude to go with it. But in Arizona, it's a whole different world from the East Coast.

I could get used to this place. Women were everywhere and no attitude. I saw six feet dimes, five feet dimes…all types of dimes. I love Arizona…I can tell you that much. There's so much money in Scottsdale, Arizona that I felt broke. I think we hit every club out there and when my cousin was checking out colleges, I hit every strip club I could find. I stayed at the finest hotels and ate like a king. I paid for me and my cousin; she was a good girl and my money was damn near free, if you know what I mean. Over the month, I spent $40,000. Shit…the hotel alone was $15,000 for the month. I rented a Porsche 911 which cost another $15,000 and I spent $10,000 on food, bars and strippers.

My next stop was Palm Beach to visit my boy, D-Man for a month. Now this was nothing like Arizona at all. This motherfucker was hood: Black people everywhere…gold teeth, dred locks…hood shit out! In this bitch, you could get a dime bag on almost every damn corner and they had clubs where you could smoke weed and shit. They would even sell you a blunt with your dime. The shit was crazy.

D-Man told me the first night, "Yo', Money…this isn't like New England where you can hang out after the club in the parking lot, cuz. These fools be bustin' shots."

That night, I found that out the hard way. The club had just closed and we were sitting by the car. I had just gotten a fly red bone's number and…*bang, bang,* you could hear the shots go off in the air. One gunshot, then another. Everyone scattered and ran for their cars. My man was right, but damn…it is still hard for me to understand that stupid shit. In the Bean (Boston), the parking lot was where you really spit your game to the hoes and even got numbers from the ones that were eyeing you that you missed out on and the ones you didn't even see.

Florida is ok and a nice place to visit, but I wouldn't want to live there. I knew that shit from the door. It was way too humid. Shit…I'd wake up with a bloody nose. I don't know how the old people do it…move to Florida to retire. Fuck that!

We hit Orlando, Miami, all over Florida. I'll give Florida this though…it had some bad bitches; especially the Cuban hoes. I spent even more dough there than I did in both other places combined. You could rent Lambos, and Ferraris. I flossed like a baller; I dropped $85,000. I can't even remember what I spent the dough on, but the cars alone were $7,500 a week so I spent $30,000 on those rentals. Shit…I was young and dumb. There have been many years since then that I wish I had that money back, but I don't regret it. It was something to remember.

It was time for me to head home and Handle My Biz. By this point, even though I still had dough, I was homesick and wanted to get my life and bank back in order. I had $115,000 left and wanted to make moves. The summer was fun, but it was time to do things. I started the semester at Hesser College in Manchester, New Hampshire. Even though I had dough, I decided to stay at the dorms. I was gonna hit the books hard and flood the school with the best weed I could find. I had met this Dominican cat named Dennis that was doing it big. He was picking up probably a thousand pounds of that killer smoke and he wanted me down with his team. I did the math. I'm pretty sure he was paying $500 a pound times one thousand; $500,000...selling it to me for $750 or $800 meant $800,000. He was making $300,000 easy. I was trying to get it like he was getting it. He was cool and all, but he was sloppy and soft. I was gonna fuck with him only as long as it took to get mine.

I was bubbling at the school and the club next to the dorms. The Pyramid was my spot. I was there Wednesday through

Saturday even though I was only eighteen. I'd hit the door and man off with smoke and skip the line of a hundred people waiting. I could always feel the haters' stares as I walked to the front and they had been waiting for a while. The bitches saw my shine, so they knew. Every once in a while, I see a couple of friends and I'd grab her hand and walk them in with me. I was a young star shining hard at the time. Shit...I had more pull than my connect at this club. In time, it wasn't long before I could see the hate in his eyes from the love I got from the bitches and the bartenders at the club. Even though he had more dough than me, he couldn't buy my looks and swag. I knew it was only a matter of time before I had to get his bitch ass, but things were going so good that that would have to wait.

I was doing well in school; with a 3.7 GPA, I was on the Dean's List. I was banging more girls than I knew what to do with. The dorm was starting to bore me though; there were too many rules. It was time to get a crib. I decided to get one with my cousin, Malik, in Nashua about twenty minutes from the school and club that I damn near ran that shit. I had pull in there like Tug of War. I had turned nineteen and my dough was stacking up. At this point, I was moving more of my connect's 1,000 pounds than he was. He couldn't even keep track. Shit...I'd get him for 10 here and there. He was so unorganized, he didn't even know; plus, he was making all that dough and it was like it made him softer and softer and definitely sloppier.

*****

Now this is going to be the part of the book where my passion, love, emotion, fear, incarceration, pain, feelings, and confusion leak out through the ink from this pen to the paper of this pad. My words will be coming deep from my heart, because believe it or not, a young pimp falls in Luv. Yup...I said, *LUV*. I remember it like it was yesterday, even though it was fifteen years ago to date as I am writing this.

It was a hot summer night. I remember getting dressed in the mirror; black jeans, black Aldo shoes with a cream Armani belt to match my cream muscle AX Armani Exchange shirt. I said a prayer before I left the house that night asking God to put someone special in my life and heart. Until that night, females were just for my pleasure and to see what I could get out of them. I had no Luv in my heart for these hoes; but this night was going to be different.

Other than the prayer, this night started the same as many others. A couple of my boys and I were heading to Guido's Night Club on Hampton Beach. It was a hot spot during the summer. They had $2 drinks and it got packed. I only drink top shelf though, but mad people came out for the cheap drinks. I grabbed my usual at the time, Henny on the rocks and a Heineken to chase it; leaving the bartender $20 and not waiting for change as I approached the dance floor. I didn't dance; shit…I had a nasty two step though, but I stood still overseeing the dance floor as women eyed me. Even dudes were commenting on the size of my traps (shoulders), which sounds weird, but I was in the best shape of my life with a lil swallow. I had been on the juice for a couple of months and boy did it show. I looked like a Black Arnold Schwarzenegger.

It was like everything slowed down...the music, the crowd; when I first laid my eyes on her, I would have thought I was drunk, but I had barely started to sip when I noticed her. For me, it was definitely Luv at first sight. She was perfect in my eyes. She was definitely Italian; I could tell by the long dark hair and the olive tan skin. Her eyes were like a cat and her face like an angel. She was dressed in all black; a shirt that showed her cleavage and arms and a mini skirt that showed her thick thighs. Her sandals showed off her perfect size five feet. She was 5'9" and should have been in a video the way she was dancing and flicking her hair. Shit...just remembering it, and writing it down, I need to pause and take a moment to get my breath back. She was a goddess; definitely a creation of God's hands.

I tried to stare her down to see if I could get eye contact. Shit...that's all I needed to pull a chick. *If you look a pimp in his eyes...it's over.* But she was smooth. The way she flicked her hair and rocked those hips, I couldn't tell if she was looking at me or through me. Damn, I don't even know how long I was staring. The music started to speed up just to slow down for me to hear the DJ say, "Last song."

She grabbed her girl's hand, whom I later I found out was her cousin, and they ran out the door. I put down the full ass drinks that I hadn't even sipped on and followed her outside and across the street to the parking lot.

I yelled out, "Excuse me. Excuse me. May I please speak to you for a moment?"

She looked me up and down and must have liked what she saw because she told her cousin that she would meet her at the car. She stood there in the moonlight looking so perfect with the sounds of the ocean to the right of me about fifty feet away.

All I could utter was, "You are put together very well."

She said, "Thank you," and it was on.

Her name was Channa; she lived in Chelmsford, Mass, about fifteen minutes from me. In my head, I thanked God for making her and allowing this to happen. I felt like a little kid as I spit my game; no…fuck that…as I *spoke* to her, because there was no game going on at all. I wanted her so badly I could feel it all through my body. She was definitely the one.

We spoke and laughed for a couple of minutes and I got her digits. After that, her cousin came back and told her that it was time to go, so I let her go and told her that she would hear from me in a couple of days. As I said the words, I tried hard to be cool, but in my heart I knew I'd call here in a day. That night as my boys and I drove home, I couldn't get Channa off my mind.

I said to them, "Damn, did you see that chick I pulled?" I was already sprung.

The next night, I called her and we spoke on the phone for hours. The convo was so good that neither one of us wanted to get off the phone. We talked till about 3:00 in the morning. The feeling that went through me the next couple of days is so hard to explain because I had never felt that way before. To this day, I still haven't felt that way. That girl will always have a part of my heart. There is nothing better than your first Luv.

Channa and I talked and chilled hard over the next couple of months; movies, dinner, clubs and tons of phone time. I even visited her at work and she spent the night. Damn...I waited until our third date before I even tried to kiss her. I had respect for her, so I didn't want to fuck it up. To this day, I know I should have married that girl; but when you are young, you don't know any better.

She was perfect in my eyes; everything I dreamed of. She had a body like Beyonce and a face and complexion like Kim Kardashian. I was truly in Luv. I couldn't wait for the time that we could both look in each other's eyes and say it at the same time. It would come...but not the way that I wanted. I was feeling good that I had someone I cared about and could see having a future with; but Luv clouds your mind and with the changes...I wasn't even aware of what was going to happen.

My old connect, Dennis, lived in the same apartment building where I lived, and he had been hating and plotting on me. I hadn't been using him as much because I had gone over his head and been fuckin' with his boy, Miguel. Miguel had the same Dominican connect as Dennis, and he was giving me product cheaper; so I was doing big things with Miguel and was about to get out of the game. One or two more moves and I would have been straight. But like they say, *it's always the last move that gets you fucked up*, and I would find that to be true more than once in my life.

While I was falling in Luv, tons of things were happening all around me. First, my so-called boy, AL, came home from school. He was playing Division One Basketball for Manhattan. We had been boys since I was thirteen; shit...we had a singing group and all about the same damn time that Boys II Men came out with "Motown Philly." I can almost still remember the dance steps that we had back in the day. But college had changed AL. He already thought he was a star. He came home broke as shit and I was doing it pushing ecstasy, coke, and weed at the time. So thinking that AL was my boy, I would hook him up with an ounce of smoke and some coke and ecstasy to trick out with the hoes; but it was getting to the point where he was knocking on the door every morning still fucked up from the night before with his hands out. He was going through an ounce of weed, twenty E pills and seven grams of coke. I didn't know if he was straight giving that shit out or using all that shit, but I wasn't going to be supporting his habits. At that point, he started to hate a little.

I was spending more and more time with my girl, when one day, AL called up and asked if I wanted to get down with a lick that he and my boy, P, were planning on robbing a movie theater that they had some inside info on. I declined because that wasn't my hustle anymore; plus, I wasn't trying to take any extra chances. Well, AL didn't take that very well and started to hate even more.

A week or so later, they tried their lick and it didn't go as planned. Their inside person had quit the job a month or so before and didn't know that there had been some changes made at the theater. After she left, the new assistant manager and an employee had started inviting their boyfriends and girlfriends in after hours and they would drink some beers, smoke a little weed and watch movies. When AL and my boy started to rob the movie theater, they did not know that sitting outside in the car, were the boyfriend and girlfriend waiting with a thirty pack to get the party started. When they noticed the two armed men dressed in all black, they called the police. By the time AL and P went to leave the building, it was surrounded. Within minutes, AL's basketball career was over. They both went to prison. P stayed there and AL got bailed out. In his eyes, his life was over, so he started to plot on me…his boy…what a friend. But I guess you gotta do what you gotta do.

Knowing that I was doing big things, AL started to show up. At that point, I felt bad for him. His dreams were over. If I only knew what he was up to, I would have never showed him luv. I had just re-upped with Miguel at the time. I spent $50,000 and he cuffed me $50,000. I had moved everything that day and had $135,000 sitting in the crib. There are always those times when you wish you did *this or that*. Well, this was one of those times.

I was going clubbing that night with my girl and AL showed up acting strange. I had previously told him my plans, and he also knew my cousin was going out for the night. We lived on the second floor with a porch with a sliding glass door. As he stood there talking to me, he kept leaning on the sliding glass door like he was waiting on something. I kept telling him that I was about to bounce and that he needed to go; then I would lock the sliding door and head in my room to get ready. Five to ten minutes would pass and I'd go out to the living room and he would have re-opened the sliding glass door. This went on three or four times. At the time I thought nothing of it; but the final time, he must have not opened the door like he had done the other time, but just unlocked it instead, so I didn't check it because I didn't see it open.

He left my place, knowing that the house was empty. The fucked up part is that I was going to the same club as my connect. I could have dropped off what I owed him, but I didn't want to drive with the cash on me and I told him I'd just meet him the next day with the money. Little did I know that the next day I would not have it.

When I came home at 3:00 am, my girl and I got to the crib and I turned the knob and the door opened and I was in shock because first, I knew I had locked the door and second, when I got to my room, I could tell someone had been there. I had been got. The $135,000 was gone; plus another $100,000. My head was spinning. I was broke. I couldn't believe it. To top it all off, I owed the Dominican cats a grip of dough. I knew there were not going to take that lightly. I didn't know what to do. I began pacing back and forth. My girl tried to comfort me, but she didn't know what to do. She had my back though.

"It's going to be alright," she said.

In my mind I was like, *yeah, right*. But it felt good that she was trying to help. While I was freaking out, guess who shows up hollering up at the window, "Yo', money. Yo' money!" Yeah, you guessed it…AL. I thought that was strange. I thought to myself, *what's he doing here?* My mind wasn't right, but I finally came to the conclusion that he had set the hit up and was trying to not only find out the status of it, but also to see if the person whom he had rob me, was telling the truth about the numbers.

Shit...I know there's no loyalty amongst thieves. When he was acting strange when he left my place before we went clubbing, the first thing my girl had said was, "I don't trust him." She was right. What AL didn't know was where I got the shit from. So when I told Miguel that I had been robbed for over $200,000 large, he called his connect to let him know what was going on. His connect told him that Dennis, my old connect that lived up stairs from me had just paid him $50,000 that he had been ducking him for, for months. Then Dennis bought another $190,000 worth of product. I knew that had to be my dough and dumb ass AL must have gotten $10,000 or so for leaving the door unlocked. I guess he got beat also.

All I could say was that I was heated. I called my cousin, Galen, who lived in Troy, New York (at Albany State) where he had started college to play football. I told him what had happened. My cousin hated when I got fucked with.

He said, "Give me the word and I will be down."

I already knew he would say that. I knew that after everything was said and done, I would have to get out of town for a while.

"Start looking for a crib for me in Upstate cause I'm about to move," I replied.

I wasn't sure what my girl was going to think, but I knew this would test her love for sure. I told Miguel that as soon as he heard something, to let me know because I was not going to let that shit slide. When I did get my payback, I just might beat Miguel too and just bounce to Upstate. I wasn't sure what I wanted to do, but my girl had made up her mind.

She said, "I'm down." That made me happy. If she was willing to give up her life for me, I was going to do the best I could do to make this work.

A couple of days later, Miguel called me and told me that he was at Dennis' crib and that he had all the work he bought underneath the bed. That was all I had to hear. I called my cousin Galen and he, Randy, Train and Damond were on their way. Four hours later, the team was back together. Whatever I was gonna get, I'd have to split with them, so my take was gonna be low; but payback was enough for me.

Dennis was soft; so I knew there wasn't going to be any problems, but I wanted to show him I had muscle to back me up, so we were going in hard. When we got there, Dennis' car was not there and I wanted him to be there for it. He had two of his cousins in the crib. We waited for a couple of hours, but Dennis didn't show and everyone was getting impatient; especially me, so I said, "Fuck it…let's go."

Randy knocked on the door. Since I lived in the building, I already had the keys for the building's entrance. When Randy knocked on the door, Dennis' cousin asked, "Who is it?"

Randy said, "It's Peter from next door," with the whitest voice ever, which was easy for Randy since he was white.

When they cracked the door a little...BANG...my cousin kicked the door, which bounced off homeboy's head and we were in like a swarm of bees with guns drawn. The two Spanish dudes gave up with no fight at all. They were duct taped within seconds and we were searching the house. Just like Miguel said, we found almost ten kilos under the bed in two suitcases. We also grabbed a safe that ended up empty.

Since the cousin, to the best of my knowledge, had nothing to do with robbing me, we didn't harm them. That took a lot of coaxing on my part since my cousin wanted to fuck someone up. He looked sad when he didn't get to go up someone's head. I gave everyone a kilo and I had six for myself. I sold them for $20,000 a piece; leaving me with $120,000. Nowhere near what I should have. Shit...I owed the Dominicans $100,000, so I decided to pack up and just leave. What happened next, I wasn't prepared for at all. I definitely didn't see it coming at all.

Miguel called my phone for two days straight. At that point, I was in a hotel in Troy, New York with my girl, sipping on that bubbly in a Jacuzzi, wondering what would be my next move. I got a call from my cousin, Malik's phone. He was the one that I had just lived with previously.

When I answered the phone, I heard Malik say, "Sorry cousin," and Miguel snatched the phone.

He said, "Yo' I got your cousin. I need my dough."

What the fuck…was all that went through my mind. Now I had more shit to handle. How stupid could my cousin be? I had told him to stay low for a little while. Why didn't he listen?

I told Miguel I was out of town, but I'd see him in the morning. Shit…I knew Miguel wasn't a killer, but I didn't know much about his connects. I knew I wasn't giving up all my dough either. I had my BMW 325 worth $18,000. I also had a brand new Jeep Cherokee worth $12,000, and I'd give another $50,000…shit that was $80,000 total; still $20,000 short, but he was going to have to take it or we could go to war. Miguel was lucky that I liked him or he would have just war. I have to give it to him, he did his part by letting me know where the work was, but I had lost a lot of dough over that shit too!

I called him back after I was sober. Shit…I didn't want to be on some *Scarface* shit…screaming crazy shit and end up getting my ass hung up on. You could tell he wasn't as happy about the whole thing as getting the whole $100,000 in cash, but he was going to take the deal. The next day, we planned on meeting at the Pheasant Lane Mall in Nashua, New Hampshire. I wanted to meet in a public place so that shit didn't get crazy. I couldn't even tell my cousin, Galen, because Malik was his brother. Galen would have killed everyone and I didn't want that drama right now. I had already been through a lot.

The next day, we were to meet at 11:00 am. I wanted to show up at 10:00 am to make sure shit was good. I had Randy drive the Beemer and Train drive the Jeep. I took my girl's Benz and I had $50,000 in a backpack with my nine cocked and loaded. All three cars parked side to side facing the entrance of the mall. Miguel showed up around 10:30 am; probably thinking the same thing about getting there early to make sure shit was cool; but I was already there and ready. He had my cousin driving shotgun and two Spanish cats with him to drive the cars back. Like I said, I always liked Miguel, he was a solid dude; but this was business, so I understood the whole cousin thing. He was lucky I didn't tell Galen because he wouldn't have taken it so lightly. Fact...the exchange went easier than selling a dime bag of weed. Even though my cousin, Malik was older than I was, I let him have it when I jumped in the car.

"What was your stupid ass thinking? I told you to lay low."

"Miguel pulled up two days ago by himself. He had a rolled blunt and said he just wanted to talk, so I jumped in the car. The next thing I knew, we were in Lawrence, Mass, eating Spanish soup sancocho at Miguel's sister's house and that's when he called you."

I couldn't believe that dumb ass pothead. After all that time, my cousin wasn't really in any harm. He was actually eating well and smoking mad blunts. *Stupid motherfucker!* One call and there would have been bodies everywhere. All I could do was shake my head. He had to work that night so he was upset about that. He didn't even know what could have really happened.

Chapter 4

I finally got a crib in Upstate New York; a four bedroom condo that cost me $2,000 a month. I had about $75,000 left to my name. I bought a Jaguar S Type to roll in and had a bad chick on my arms. I was going to enjoy it for a little while. I knew sooner or later, I'd have to make moves; but for now, it was time to enjoy life. First, I planned a vacation back to California to visit my cousin. My girl had never been there before, so we were going to hit Vegas and California for a week each. To tell you the truth, the next six months or so were the happiest I had ever been. Channa was an angel sent from heaven; like they say, *you don't know what you have till it is gone.*

We were doing well though. When we got back from vacation, she started to get a little home sick, so I brought her a cat. We named it Guido after the club we first met at. It was a Siamese cat. I hate cats, but I grew up around Siamese; plus, I once read they were known to guard Egyptians temples back in the day, so I dropped $400 on it.

You learn a lot about people when you live with them. Like the fact that Channa didn't change the kitty litter. It made her sick. I guess her mom used to do it when she had one as a child. I wish I had known that before I bought that damn cat; but it was alright, Channa did so much other stuff that it was worth it. She cooked, she cleaned, she did the laundry and the sex was amazing. Damn...she was nice to just look at. She didn't have to do shit; it was a bonus the shit she did.

I was truly in Luv. The only problem was that I was young and had pimping running through my veins. I had never been faithful; and I was trying so hard. Galen had moved in with us and was always trying to get me to go out. Like a smart girl, Channa wasn't having that shit. So, little by little, I was starting to feel blocked in; but I was still holding my cool. She got a job bartending, and I started to make moves again. I was driving back to Mass to reup and back to New Hampshire to unload and then back home to Upstate New York. I was grabbing $5,000 to $10,000 of ecstasy at a time. I was doing alright even though I was driving with no license; I had lost my license for speeding. But when you are young, there's no fear in your heart. You think you are invincible. When you are in Luv, you feel the same way, so I thought I was Superman. All the love songs finally meant something to me. Jon B, Craig David, Case, R. Kelly, and Donnel Jones had me on cloud nine back then. As they say, Carpe Diem (seize the moment) because things were going to change soon, but for that moment it was still fine and we were still in love.

I was dealing with this goofy dude in Upstate named George. He would always buy like 100 hundred E pills and rent a limo for two weeks straight and have ten stripper bitches partying with him. He was too goofy to be a pimp and he wasn't a drug dealer; he would just give the pills to those chicks to hang out with him. He was always trying to get me to roll with him, but I had a girl; I wasn't 'bout it. Every two weeks it was like clockwork; then the third week he would come and be broke and ask me to cuff him 50 E pills; but he would pay me for the 100. Shit...I'd already made a grip off of him, so I'd do it and a couple of days later, he would come through, pay what he owed and buy 100 more.

I'd ask him how he was getting his dough and he would always say, "You don't want to know. You wouldn't want to do it," and then he would just smile.

My cousin and I would tell him we were down, and he would always just laugh it off. This went on for months and I still had no clue what that nigga did for his money. Well one day, the Feds came knocking at the door asking questions and saying that a couple of banks had been robbed and the getaway car was seen coming in our complex. Shit, I didn't know anything about it. I was too busy worrying about the 6,000 E pills I had hiding in the heating vent, but when the Feds left and I watched them knock at all the other doors, I stopped worrying as much, but I still moved my stash. Three days later, I walked in the crib and Galen was laughing like crazy.

He says, "You're not going to believe this shit!" and points at a newspaper on the table.

He was right. I couldn't believe my eyes. In big, bold printing it said,

FORMER TRACK STAR ARRESTED FOR OVER 15 BANK ROBBERIES.

George's picture was underneath the heading. That fool was a robbing banks, gangster ass nigga. I guess you can't judge a book by its cover. Other than getting caught, he was smart about it. He had a fake gun with a wooden handle with tape, so it wasn't armed robbery. Slick little nigga; that small detail saved him twenty years or so on his sentence. He was a star in high school in the 100 meter dash and he used that to his advantage as well. He would park the car two blocks away and after he hit the bank teller for the money, that little nigga was ghost. Now that's how you *Handle Ur Biz*. But he still ended up getting a seven and a half to fifteen year sentence. The strange but good thing was that he did ten years and became a pastor and now he helps young people make better decisions with their life. Now that's even more gangsta real talk.

Well, back to me and my girl...for my twenty-second birthday, she bought tickets for me and her to go to Barbados for a vacation and to maybe find my dad. That's some G shit. Like I said, I will always have Luv for that girl. She knew how to Handle Her Biz. I love Barbados; the singer, Rihanna, is from there. Me and my girl had an all-inclusive stay at a hotel on the beach. We rented a car and I had her do all the driving because the steering wheel was on the other side of the car and you had to drive on the other side of the road. She had been to Africa, so she was able to whip the shit out of the rental; I was too high and drunk most of the time to fuck with that. My father was a legend on the island, so it wasn't too hard to find him. When we took the cab from the airport, I asked the cab driver if he knew a guy named Clyde.

He said, "Big Clyde?"

I replied, "Shit, I guess so. I only met him once, so I don't know for sure. I was only seven when I met him, so everyone was big to me at that time."

The cab driver told me that Clyde owned a taxi company and that he drove tourists around and that I could find him by the pier where the boats came in. It took us almost the whole trip to find him. We would get an address from someone and when we got there, they would say that he moved a month or so ago, but after a couple of wild goose chases, we found him. We pulled up to this house and he happened to be walking out. I walked up to him and asked if he was Clyde. I could tell right away that he was my father. He had the same eyes as me; very light brown with a hazel tint. I hadn't seen very many people, especially brothers, with eyes like mine.

"Why you want to know?" he asked.

"Do you know a lady named Dede from the states?" That was my mom's nickname, but it was also what she went by.

"Yes."

"She told me that you were my dad."

He hugged me right away and I could see my girl in the car crying. Shit...she was the one that made this happen. She was happy to be part of the moment and I was happy that she was happy because I never would have done it by myself.

We were supposed to leave the next day, but he invited us to stay with him for a little bit. We changed our tickets and stayed a week longer. He showed us the island and we searched for the state's animal...a green monkey. He knew the island like the back of his hand. I had a lot of questions for that man. We sat for hours and he explained a lot to me. He told me that he asked my mom to marry him when I was seven and he said he understood why she didn't. He said that he was so deep in the game and it was good that she didn't because a couple of years after we left, his whole life changed. He was now living in a very modest home with three regular taxi cabs. All the Benzes and soldiers were gone.

The more he talked, the more I began to realize that he still had some pimp in him. At forty-eight years old, he was dating a nineteen-year-old swimsuit model. I also had brothers because he had two baby mommas on the island. He told me that he had hung the pimp game up and the drug game also. He said that he was dealing with some serious dudes back in the day and his shipments were a couple of million each. He went on to say that when shipment after shipment got seized, he lost his millions and started to be in debt and owed his connect ten million. Since he had been in business so long with his connects, they gave him a choice; either walk away from the game or work to pay the debit off.

"I had lost a lot of soldiers and family due to the game, so I wanted to start over and they were giving me the chance to do so, so I did it."

At the point I was in my life, I didn't blame him. I think maybe I would have done the same thing if given the opportunity.

"I have no regrets, although I do miss the power though," he said.

Then he showed me album after album of pictures of him doing his thing. In one of the pictures he was standing on top of five million dollars with bad bitches laying on the ground butt ass naked. In another picture he was standing on top of a Benz with twenty armed soldiers standing on each side of him. He was *Handling His Biz* for sure.

Me and Channa stayed for a couple of days and then we went back to the states. When we got back, a lot of things started to change. I loved that girl with all my heart, but I was so young that I was starting to feel trapped. We started fighting a lot over nothing. Then her mother became sick which didn't help the situation. After a year or so, she moved back to Mass and I stayed in Upstate New York. As much as I missed her, but that is when my pimping really began.

Chapter 5

My money was at an all-time low, but that didn't hold me back. First, I bagged an Asian chick. Now that bitch was bad. She taught me a couple of things about the game. We hit Connecticut, Rhode Island and New Jersey. I stacked a good $10,000 in a couple of weeks. One thing I learned from fucking with her is that hoes come and go. She started to use drugs hard over the couple of weeks that we were together and that made the bitch very bipolar; plus, I was missing Channa bad. I at least wanted to be around her while her mom was dying; that was the least I could do. I knew we were not going to last because I wanted to get my foot in the pimp game.

The streets were pulling me in harder than ever. I needed a lil bit more dough if I was going back to Mass. So I was already plotting on a couple of licks in Upstate. One white boy that I had been fucking with was going to be an easy mark and a quick $15,000 to add to my stash. He was looking to grab a lot of E pills and was quick to hand over the cash and go for a ride.

We drove to Malden, my home town. If you were from Malden, you knew the layout. They had these steps in downtown that lead to an arcade. You couldn't see all the way down the steps from the street, but at the end of the steps, you could go right to get to the arcade, or left to an alleyway that lead you to the middle of downtown Malden. So the lick was easy. The fool handed me $15,000 and I simply walked away with it with my cousin Lloyd waiting on the other side with a blunt rolled. By the time the fool noticed that I wasn't coming back, I was already picking out new furniture for my new apartment.

I spent the next couple of months trying to be there for Channa while her mom slowly died. It was a damn shame. Her mother was a nice lady; didn't drink, smoke or eat meat. She caught a rare case of Cancer that killed her slowly.

While I was getting deep in the game, I had linked up with a pimp named Shane that I knew from my childhood. His mom and my mom were cool back in the day; running the streets hard. Now Shane was a real ass pimp. I would call him the Michael Jordan of the game. I'm no homo, but Shane was *The Man*. His whip game was crazy; a Range Rover, a Lexus, a Benz 500, a Benz 600, a BMW 325, a BMW 740, and a ILL motorcycle. That dude would pull up and be worth $100,000 in minks, blinged out, throwback jerseys, and $600 to $700 in True Religion Jeans. He had anywhere from ten to fifteen chicks working for him at a time. He would have those bitches sleeping on bunk beds and shit.

One night, he called me up, he wanted two ounces of smoke; even though he barely smoked, drank, or gambled, he wanted it for his chicks. He asked me to meet him and go for a ride to Foxwoods. He had to pick up money from a chick that was trying to get on his team. The chick had set up something with some rich business man. We arrived at Foxwoods and he just went into pimp mode. That nigga had the glow like Bruce Leroy did when he fought Sho'nuff...true talk.

He went off on her, "Bitch, where the fuck are you at? You got me walking around this casino like Joe Flippa head!"

I could hear the chick pleading with him, "Daddy, I'm at the food court."

"Bitch, there's like ten food courts in here. Now which fuckin' one!"

We finally found her and there were two of them. One was his main bitch and the other one was the one that set it up and was trying to get on the team. The main chick was bad; about 5'8", 120 pounds, dark hair, and a bangin' body. I could tell she worked out, and she had a face like Angelina Jolie. Shit…I'd wife the bitch. My first thought was, *Damn, she's too sexy to be selling her pussy.* Now the second chick was a little shorter and had some big ass tits and big ass lips. My first thought was, *I'd let that bitch suck my dick.* She just had the face and lips for it.

They handed him $4,000 and went back to the crib, they both had to wake up early to do more work. It's funny…married guys will lie to their wives and say they are going to the gym or have to go in to work early so that they can trick out. It works though because their wives are not thinking that their husbands are getting pussy or cheating at 7:00 in the morning, but they are so wrong. A lot of shit in the pimp game is early. The early bird catches the worm.

"What did they do to get that four Gs," I asked Shane.

"My main bitch fucked for a couple of hours while the other one was sucking dick for a couple of hours."

Guess I was on point about the shorter one's lips. It was nice being with Shane. He taught me a lot, but like any true pimp, they are not going to teach you everything.

Another time, Shane and I met at The Roxy in Boston. He had all his bitches out on that night; about fourteen of them. You should have seen that dude. He had all the chicks dressed in white everything. All the bitches ranged from a nine to a ten on a scale of one to ten. He had all his whips shining and parked in the parking lot; side by side. When the club let out and the parking lot was packed, he made all fourteen chicks wipe down the rims on the cars. Like the white boys say, *That shit was epic*! Just think about it. Fourteen hot ass white girls dressed in all white, bent over, dusting the rims on nice ass cars while Shane stood there with a smirk on his face like, *Top that!*

The whole parking lot froze. You could see nigga's envy and hate. You could hear other bitches talking shit like, "I'd never" and "Oh my God" but it didn't faze Shane. He knew what he was doing. His pimp hand was strong and his game was tight. I wanted that life bad! Like I said in the beginning...I didn't have lawyers and doctors to look up to. I had this. Pimping. Any chance I got, I hung with Shane just to try to get a little of his pimping to rub off on me and to learn what I could from him.

During that time, I had met a couple of chicks that he would buy off of me. $1,500 a pop wasn't bad. He could do more with them than I could; plus, I was a pimp in training. I wanted to learn everything I could before I went head first in the game; but I had a little set back. Remember when I said that my cousin, Tia had told me, "Never base on a crackhead." Well, I guess I forgot that because I was dealing with a dude named Scott and he had cuffed

$200 bucks work of crack off me and then he disappeared for two weeks.

When he came back, he just showed up at my door early in the morning saying, "I don't have any of the money I owe you, but I need to buy $150 worth."

I snapped. "I should stomp the shit out of you, take that $150, and cut my loss," which is exactly what I should have done.

He was in his forties and he took my remarks as me being disrespectful to him, so he left my house thinking, *I'm going to teach this cocky nigga a lesson.* I know you are probably thinking, *This dude talking all that big money shit, yet he is cuffing $200 worth of crack.* Well, I was a real hustler when I was in the game. Shit...I took change, nickels, dimes, and quarters. I took iPods, clothes with tags still on them, TVs, and anything else I could make money off of. I would be sitting on a kilo and still sell dimes and nicks. I was about that money and the stuff that I couldn't sell I gave away to family members or friends.

Well, Scott came back a couple of days later and had $100 for me and bought a $100, but what I didn't know was that it went straight to the police. They were on to me and I didn't even know it. The next couple of days, I went on with business like I would normally do. It's funny...after you get popped, you start to think about shit that you noticed right before shit went down. Like the old white man sitting in the parking lot reading a newspaper two days in a row. Things like that cross your mind; but you don't put two and two together at the time. You only remember them after it's too late.

A couple of days passed, and Scott was back with the $100 he owed me and another $100 to spend, but that time, he asked me to split the $100 into two bags. One he put in his sock and the other one, he kept for himself. Again, I thought nothing of what he was doing until afterwards. I just thought to myself that he just beat someone and was keeping some for himself. In reality, he did keep some for himself and the rest went to the police again. God was on my side thought, the eight ounces of coke that I had left, I got rid of that night and kept a half gram for some stripper I was fucking with.

The next day when I woke up, I remembered that I left my Garcia Vega in the car. I wanted to smoke my morning blunt, so I walked to the car and so the right of me I saw ten police in SWAT gear. I hoped they weren't there for me, but the fifth cop in line must have been a rookie because he tried to hide like I couldn't see the other nine copes. I knew there were there for me, so I kept walking to my car thinking about what I had left in the crib: half a gram of coke, two ounces of weed, four bottles of steroids, twelve hypodermic needles, and $15,000 in cash – which the cops only listed as $7,500.

I was hit. It was my first charge. People talk all that gangster shit; but truth be told, I didn't know what was going to happen. So many thoughts go through your mind when you get busted. Like…Who snitched? How many sales do they have? Can I get bailed out?

I was shook. I had money on the streets, but shit was going to be different now. I knew that for a fact. My bail was only a $40 P.R. bail because it was out of Mass. I bailed out the same day and collected all the money owed to me; $20,000, which went straight to a lawyer. Well, $13,000 did. The rest I had to find a new car and switch whips. I was fucked up in the game.

At this point, I had been fucking with one of my old connects from P.O.D. (Posse of Destruction) from when I was ten years old. Now tony was a true G that I could trust; an Italian dude that grew up in the same projects that I had. He had really come up in the game. He had game, he could have even pimped, but he was always on some, "I'll leave that up to the brothers…White guys aren't pimps" shit. I knew he trusted me, but I couldn't tell him I just got busted. It's business. Shit…he wouldn't want to fuck with me at that time, so I didn't tell him. I just told him that money was tied up and I needed twenty to thirty pound of weed to make a move. Tony hooked me up with no questions asked. I got rid of all thirty pounds that same day and made a quick $6,000. The next day, I went and paid him his dough and told him what had really happened to me and that I was going to chill for a bit. He understood and told me if I needed anything to hit him up. Like I said, Tony was a true G. He always stayed with his money stacked up, always had a fly bitch, a phat car and a nice crib. I had a lot of respect for him. He is another person that taught me a lot in the game. He was about his paper; always on the top of his game.

Over the next year, a lot of things changed for me. I had always said to myself that if I caught a case, I was out of the game. But it doesn't work that way. You end up deeper in the game. I needed to make dough. I still owed my lawyer another $7,000. It was going to cost me $20,000 for him alone, plus I still had to live.

I moved from Lowell, Mass, back to Nashua, New Hampshire while I was going to court. I made moves here and there, but slowed down a lot. Channa and I were falling apart, little by little. I loved her, but I had to deal with the bullshit I was dealing with and I didn't want to drag her down with me. I had a couple of chicks that I was fucking with, and I was making a little money in the pimp game, but I wasn't trying to catch another case while I was out on bail. So, even that slowed down.

My lawyer told me that since everything was taking place in Mass, I wouldn't see any jail time for my first offense, but when I got arrested, my crib was 100 feet from a school zone, which was a two-year mandatory sentence. I ended up with two years of probation, which was all fucked up because since I moved, I had to transfer my probation to New Hampshire. I found out real quick that New Hampshire Probation Officers don't play. They wanted me to work. Plus, I kept pissing dirty. I had only been on probation for two months and I was going to be in violation of my probation if I kept that up. I was young and kept pushing my PO. I was hanging out in strip clubs in Mass a lot; King Arthurs, Squire in Revere and Golden Banana to name a few. I was trying to find me a bitch that was down for whatever, and I was trying to keep my face out of the city where my probation was.

I was still moving fast. I needed to slow my ass down. When I look back, I don't know what I was thinking. I was caught up in the life hard. At the same time, someone put me on to a Haitian dude named Razor. He had kilos for super low. I normally didn't mess with new connects, but I was off my game bad. What I didn't know was that Razor was robbing mad people. The most that would happen to him if he got caught was that he would get deported, so he was crazy with his. He was plotting on me hard. I bought one kilo at first for $15,000. He knew what he was doing. He told me that the more I bought, the cheaper it would be. He would drop down to $10,000 if I grabbed four, so I worked my way up...one, then two, then three, then four. I was using other people's money and I'd just take mine off the top. I normally met him in a parking lot. He never drove. He was always with someone else in a car with them driving. He would jump in my ride and have the bag between his legs and place it on the floor.

For the latest meeting, I thought everything would go the same, but when he jumped in the car, all I could smell was food. Since he was Haitian, I assumed the smell was just him. I handed him the $40,000 and let him jump out. Something told me to check the bag, and I did. It was full of empty food containers. I just got beat!

Razor jumped in the passenger side of a Durango. I floored the Honda I was driving. Mind you…I didn't have a license, a gun, and I was on probation. I was living recklessly. I chased them through Everett, Mass, and then my hometown of Malden before slamming into the Durango and knocking off my bumper. While I was on the cell trying to get a couple of my boys to cut Razor off, that's when I noticed a chrome nine come out the passenger window. When we hit a side street, *Blocka Blocka*…the nine went off. The Honda took two hits to the front; stopping it in its place. If the shots had been a little higher, they would have come through the windshield. As I thought about it, when Razor was in the car with me, if I had of checked the bag, I could have gotten shot then; so I had really dodged death twice that night.

I jumped out of the car. Since it was just an old car that I used to go to the gym in and to make plays, it only had the basics to it. It didn't have power locks, so I locked all the doors by hand

and started to walk to meet up with my boys. My mind was going crazy. I was definitely slipping. I didn't know where that dude lived and I didn't know where he hung. I had just gotten "got" just like I had done to many other people. *What the fuck was going on? Was it Karma or should I just charge it to the game?* I just wanted to get back home and think about my next move.

My boy picked me up and drove me back to New Hampshire. I drank a bottle of Grey Goose to the head and passed out. The next morning I woke to my cell going off. It was a Mass number. I answered it and a deep male voice spoke.

"Is this *****?"

"Yes."

"Oh, you're lucky. You almost got clapped last night."

"Who is this," I said.

"It's Detective Saldano with the Everett Police Department."

"What is this about?"

He said, "We found your car."

I played stupid. "Oh, you did. That's great. Last night I walked into 7 Eleven and when I came out, it was gone. I didn't call the police because I didn't have any insurance and was so angry that I just went home. I was going to call today."

He said, "Well, I'd like to see you when you come to pick the car up, and you might want to come up with a better story because whoever stole your car locked all the doors for you!"

After saying that, he hung up. *Shit...the car can stay there for all I care*, is what I thought.

Ten minutes later, Saldano called back and said, "Oh, you're on probation in New Hampshire. Well, I just got off the phone with the head Probation Officer, so why don't you go tell them your story."

Damn man...what the fuck, is all I was thinking. My brain was spinning. It hadn't even been a full twenty-four hours since I had just checked in with my PO and she was yelling at me because my piss was dirty and I didn't have a job. How the fuck was I going to explain this? I took my damn time to go see her. I drank a gallon of water to sober up from the bottle of Grey Goose that I drank when I got home just eight hours before. Shit…I was still drunk. When I got there, her face said it all, but I gave her the same bullshit story that I gave the Detective and it worked; other than the fact that she gave me an 8:00 pm curfew.

Since my original charge was out of Lowell, I had the choice to move back there, so that's the choice I made. I just needed to find a crib. I began to grind hard for the next week and a half, found a crib and made some dough while still making my curfew. It was tough, but I did it. I was back to living in Lowell with the Mass probation and that was much easier for me. I had a year and a half left and I needed to make some changes in my life. I didn't know where to start, so I went to the only place I could really think and relax…the strip club.

My life was out of control; my luck was not good. I really didn't know which way to go. I was too deep in the game to stop and I was on probation, so I needed to be careful. I decided to lay low for the next couple of months and made small plays here and there to keep money in my pocket. I stayed at different bitches' houses trying to stay away from my crib. I missed Channa a lot, but my pride would not let me call her, so I just kept doing me.

I was hanging with Shane a lot more trying to suck up any info possible about the game. We took a couple trips to Atlantic City where I could see the master in action. He was good at what he did. We were there for a weekend or two and he was always on point; no drinking, no smoking, no gambling…he was about his money. I liked that about him. He took this shit serious. He would tell me a good chick can make $1,000 easy a night; a great chick can make a couple Gs. Like they say, *Pimping ain't easy*, and that's the truth. Dealing with girls, the tricks, and the game can stress a brother out; but he was always cool. I knew there was a lot that I could learn from him. I'd ask him all types of questions like…*How much do they get? Do you tell them you love them? Do you have sex with them?*

To my surprise, he would always answer me, but often he would just say, "It's a different game for every bitch."

He was right. You had to come at them in all types of ways to make things happen.

When I first started trying to do things by myself, things didn't always go smooth; that's for sure. This one time, I had a bad bitch, Tiffany; she was a ten in many ways. She was Italian, slim, nice little titties, a nice ass, all tanned up, dark, long hair with gold streaks in it and a very sexy style about her. She always wore fitted clothes with cleavage showing. She knew how to get a man's attention. Her baby daddy was a pimp, so she knew the game. She was a hoe and wasn't ashamed of it either.

I fucked with her for a couple of weeks and we had our fun; but like they say...*You can't turn a hoe into a housewife*, so after our little fling, we were still cool. *Don't hate the player; hate the game.* And we could both play with the best of them.

Tiffany called me up one day and said she had another girl that was willing to make money also. Over the years, I had so many girls call me up or come to me saying that they were down to do whatever, that I had lost count. Truth be told, I really think I attract crazy females. Always have. Always will. Well, this second girl was hot also; a rare combination of Asian and Spanish heritage. She had a nice body and a pretty face, but she did something that to this day I will never understand. She would shave her eyebrows off and draw them back on. I don't know what women are thinking when they do that dumb shit. But I was going to try to make money with them no matter what.

I told them to just bring some clothes with them and they could change at my cousin's house in Malden. My cousin, Patricia, was a female playa; she had four kids, but she knew how to get hers. She was a MVP; always having white boys buying her anything she wanted and she wouldn't give it up. She was slick; and they weren't buying her cheap shit either. She was getting washers and dryers, gold, diamonds new couch sets with big screen TVs, cars and all types of fly shit. I'd always stop off at her crib; it was a way to show off my different hoes and I could visit my little cousins. Plus, Malden is in the middle of everything. We were going to hit a strip club in Chelsea, Mass called King Arthurs and meet up with a pimp I knew named Riz; then we were going to Foxwoods Casino to try to make some money. The night started off good enough with everyone being in a good money making mode. When we got to my cousin's house, you could smell fried fish from the door. I didn't think anything of it. My cousin was always cooking. She had to with four kids; plus, she had four older brothers that knew where to get a plate of food. Everyone knows how Black people do.

The bathroom they were going to change in was connected to the kitchen. That fish smelled so damn good that we would have had a plate, but we were all sipping Henny on the way down and that fish would have had our stomachs fucked up. While they were changing, I spoke to my cousin for a while and then went out front to smoke a Black & Mild and to get my mind right for the night.

Just like all bitches…it took the girls about forty-five minutes too long to get ready. Finally, they were done. I said goodbye to my fam and we were on our way to the strip club. We walked through the first part of the club where the pool tables and Keno were, then in the main part where the girls were. I sat there at the bar and laid $40 bucks down. Then I told them what I wanted and went to look for my boy.

As I was walking around, a stripper passed me spraying a can of Febreze saying out loud, "Who the fuck just came in this bitch smelling like a goddamn fisherman platter?"

You should have seen the look on Tiffany's and the other girls' faces. It took the fight right out of them. They were ashamed. I should have cut my losses then; but I was money hungry. The whole night went downhill after that. There were mood swings. The two girls started to argue and fight. The one with the drawn on eyebrows started to cry and I still pushed them to go to Foxwoods thinking it would get better. $80 in gas, $50 at the bar, $40 in smoke, and $30 on a bottle of Henny...I was down $200, so I was going to try and make my money back at least.

Well, it didn't work that way at all. They just fought more and more and argued more and more. Tiffany said something about the other girl's kids and it was on. I had to pull over to pull those bitches apart. We finally got to Foxwoods, but getting out the car was even a waste of time; those bitches couldn't have made money at that point even if I paid them. The night was a bust. Shit...it didn't get any better until the ride home when I just said, "Fuck it" and got drunk and started to crack jokes. I had lost $200 and both the bitches like that! To this day, me and Tiffany are still cool, but we have never tried to make money together again.

Pimping 101. I left the house with two bad bitches and got home at 5:00 am $200 broker than when I left with no bitches. Pimping ain't easy.

Chapter 5

I was going to take a break from pimping for a while. That shit was stressful as shit. I was talking to this young eighteen-year-old girl named Raquel. She was Lebanese. She had her own crib, drove an Acura and was going to cosmetology school and working at a bar. I had six or seven months left on my probation, so I decided to just set up shop at her crib. Shit...she was never home anyway. To me, it was going to be a temporary thing; at least that's how it started. I still had my crib in Lowell for my probation, so I could always do me when I wanted to.

She was born in D.C., so she had a little swag to her. The more I hung out with her, the more she grew on me. She was young, but she had an old soul. She didn't smoke weed, but she would drink a little. We sat up many nights talking and sipping. She would sell a couple of bags of whatever for me to the girls at her job and school. I have to admit...I liked her hustle between school and work. She was putting in like eighty hours a week. The crib she lived in was in the hood. I felt right at home, but I knew sooner or later something was going to happen. It was a four-family house, and there were always little broke ass thugs hanging out front.

I was always walking in the crib with a case of Heinekens, a bottle of Hennessy, and half a dozen blunt wraps. I was chillin' on a daily basis with more than those little niggas had in their pockets combined and I could see that they were hungry. I tried to put a couple of them on, but some mutherfuckers just can't make money. One by one, they would fuck up and I don't do biz that way.

It was simple, "Here's a cell phone with minutes on it. Here's $200 worth...you keep $100 and give me back $100. Now, if you fuck that up, you need to hang it up. You're not a drug dealer."

I went through four or five of those little niggas before I gave up. Raquel and I were doing good. She gave me my space and I gave her hers. I wasn't sure what I was going to do with her, but like they say...*Everything happens for a reason.*

My probation ended. I did my two years without a violation or getting arrested. I decided to give up my crib and move in with

Raquel. We got along well. I wasn't worried about anything, even though I saw it coming.

One night we went out clubbing and one of those dirty niggas broke in the crib. He didn't get much, and I knew exactly who had broken in. It was a hating ass crackhead dude named stinky. I had two issues with the dude. First, he was a crackhead; second, he was broke. The little shit he had gotten, was already spent or smoked up; so sending in the team to rob his ass wasn't going to work, and just fucking him up wasn't going to work either. He was a crackhead, so he would have just woke up every morning plotting on how to get me back. I was making paper...things were going good. I didn't need that little petty shit in my life.

I was thinking about moving twenty minutes north of where we were. I knew that shit was going to happen before I got hit. I felt like it was my fault. I couldn't just leave Raquel in that crib alone because I started to care about her. I wasn't in Luv, but like I told her...*I had love for her.*

Because of my feelings for her, I had to take her with me. I felt bad that she had to move, so I was going to make it as easy as possible. I paid for the movers and got a little one-bedroom and paid six months' worth of rent. I told Raquel to just worry about school and I'd take care of the rest. She was a good girl, but just like with Channa, I was still deep in the game with both dealing and pimping. I could stop both for a little while, but they both kept pulling me back in. My history was that I would tell myself that I was done with the pimping, and then two weeks later, a down ass bitch would pop up; and that's exactly what happened when Raquel and I moved.

I hadn't drank or smoked in two weeks. I was hitting the gym and spending all my extra time with Raquel. One night, I decided to go to the club for a little while. Raquel was at work. I was chillin' on the dance floor overlooking the club and a chick walked up to me. She was slim; about 105 pounds with double D tits. I could tell they were fake right away. They were too big for her small frame, but they looked good. She was a seven or eight on my scale. She asked what I was drinking and if she could buy me a drink. I walked her to the bar, shot the shit with her for a couple of minutes and got her math. She looked like a stripper that I had fucked back in the day. Her name was Stephanie.

A couple of days later, I came across her number and decided to call her. Right away, I could tell she was a wild one and that she also stripped. I swear I only attract crazy chicks and strippers and she was both. We hit it off right away on the phone and decided to hang out. This chick was doing her thing. She drove a bubble Lexus and she didn't have a license. She was a reckless one. She lived with an old White man that bought her the car. She wasn't stupid. She had the title of the car in her name. The old White dude was loaded. He had twenty or thirty Acers with four-wheelers and all that shit with no say so over what she did. She ran the old man for sure.

We chilled out at his crib for the day. For a 105 pound chick, Stephanie could drink. She went through a eighteen-pack of Coors Lite in a couple of hours and wasn't even drunk. She was wild;

that's what attracted me to her at first. Raquel was a lot more conservative, so being with Stephanie was a change of pace. I knew it was going to lead to trouble fucking with her, but sometimes I let the game pull me in like that and didn't even notice as it was being done. Right off the rip, I started to make money with this chick, and that's what really had me. Like they say...*Money over bitches; M.O.B.* But when you can do both...money and bitches...that's when I'm hooked like a crackhead.

This chick had her own little stripper company and the dude she was fuckin' with got locked up for old warrants and shit. He was going to be gone for like two years. I slid into his spot like it belonged to me. That same weekend, she had three parties set up and broke me off with half. $1,000 just for being there; plus she got rid of an ounce of that white all bagged up, so that was another $1,000 profit. So within seventy-two hours of knowing that chick, I was up $2,000. I could have sworn I just told myself that I was going to chill; but that was what would always happen to me. It's like I couldn't get away from the game, even when I tried.

I was spending less and less time at home. I knew Raquel noticed, but I always kept Sundays open for her like that was enough. Girls are not stupid. They notice things; especially when they are in love with your ass. Stephanie was starting to bring me in more and more money; plus, it was fun hanging with her crazy ass. I never knew what was going to pop off.

Soon it was every other Sunday with Raquel and I was barely at the crib. I felt bad, but I thought since I was paying the bills that would be enough. Money can't buy everything though. Raquel was starting to get a little upset. She started to snoop around a little like any female would. She knew the life I lived, but I had promised to slow down when we moved. The fucked up thing was that I had planned on it, but shit like this always caught me up: the game, the life, the money, the power, and the bitches. When I would try to spend more time with Raquel, Stephanie would sense it and get into some type of problem or blow up my phone. Even though I could not control her crazy ass, I wasn't ready to let my little gold mine go. That little game of Stephanie's went on for a couple of months. I knew, little by little, that I was losing Raquel, but she was a down as bitch. She was going to stick around. Stephanie, on the other hand, was fuckin' nuts. We had a revolving cycle where I'd spend the night and in the morning she would be so crazy acting that I'd go home to Raquel and spend time with her until she left for school. Then I would smoke a blunt and get my piece of mind. Like clockwork, after a few hours, Stephanie would call and say that she was sorry and for me to come back. Then she would always say that she had food in the crockpot, a blunt rolled, a bottle ready and that she wanted to suck my dick all day. She would even add that I could treat her like a slut and fuck her in the ass till I was tired.

I don't know about you...but I can't say no to that. She would get me back at her crib every time. A couple of days later, though, it would end with a bang just like I knew it would. I just thought I would be able to be smarter and smoother each time it happened, but when you are dealing with a bipolar, crazy, stripper, it doesn't happen like that.

She was up all night getting drunk. I was trying to explain to her that I couldn't spend every night with her, that I had other things to handle and that I didn't like to be locked down. I told her that I'd stay the night, but that we needed to slow down. She didn't like that at all. She stayed on the phone all night complaining to her girls or her mother…probably both. I could hear her in the living room crying and complaining. Her voice was starting to get on my nerves. I knew there wasn't much more of her that I could handle. I planned on waking up in the morning and bouncing, then slowly cutting her off so her crazy ass couldn't do something crazy toward me.

The next morning when I woke up, I couldn't find the keys to my Beemer and when I walked into the living room, she was sitting in a chair rocking back and forth. I could tell she hadn't slept all night. She had a crazy ass look on her face.

"Have you seen my keys?" I asked.

"Yes, I know where they are, but you can't have them until we talk," she replied.

"We can talk, but not until after I went back to my crib and showered and grabbed some more weed."

She wasn't having that shit at all, and I wasn't having any of her crazy ass temper tantrums. I started to get more and more angry. I walked outside to try to cool off, but she followed me. She was going on and on about hell knows what. At that point, I just stated, "Bitch, give me my keys."

I wouldn't dare threaten to smack her because that would just show her a good time; she was *that* type of crazy, and doing something like that was just what she wanted. So instead, I had one of those plastic Gatorade bottles; it was full and I chucked it at the back of her Lexus. I thought it was going to bounce off, but it didn't. The cap, plus the force of my throw, shattered the car window. SMASH...hundreds of pieces of glass went everywhere. The look on her face was evil. That bitch cut me with her eyes like she knew she had me. I knew I was never getting my keys back. She went from wanting to talk to wanting blood.

"Nigga, you better fix my shit!" she screamed with fire in her eyes.

At that point it was as if God was crying for me because it started to rain. It was Sunday, so I knew I wasn't getting anyone out there to fix that window that day. I covered the window with trash bags and started calling around. The cheapest repair I found was for $1,300, but no one could come out for a couple of days. I had shit to do; plus, I couldn't stay there with that crazy ass bitch looking at me like she wanted to kill me. I had to get out of there.

I had a spare set of keys at my crib. I called my boy to come and get me. I had a couple of things at her crib, but I was going to have to cut my losses. If I had tried to grab anything, I knew my car would have been fucked up by the time I got back.

My boy came to scoop me up, we went and got my keys and I came back and grabbed my whip. I knew I had to sell that car because she was the type that if she saw it anywhere in the future, she would drive that shit into a lake. I wanted nothing else to do with that bitch. Fuck her window. I was going to be ghost.

That bitch blew up my phone leaving fucked up messages every day for about two months. She was out of her fuckin' mind. Just when I thought it was over, she somehow found out where Raquel worked and harassed her. To this day, I still feel bad for all the drama Raquel had to go through because of her love for me, but she would deal with that and much more over the years fuckin' with me.

Once again, I wanted to take a break from hoes and the game; but it never works that way for me though. I started to spend more time with Raquel again, trying to patch things up. Things were going good until one of my boy's birthdays came up and he wanted a few of us to go out for the night. The first stop of the night was going to be a strip club. I don't know what it is about strippers and strip clubs and me…but we fit.

Ten minutes after being there, a couple of strippers sat down and one of them was a dime. She was a Portuguese stripper named

Honey. That chick was bad; all tanned up, long black hair, real nice titties, nothing fake on her body, a very beautiful face and nice eyes. She was fine. We clicked right from the start.

"I have a man, but it's not working out," she said.

I followed suit, "I have a girl too, but it isn't working out either," I said in an old pimp move. "There's nothing like two people going through a hard relationship together; if anything, we can be friends and complain to each other."

At least, that's what I wanted her to think. I knew how to play it. She was going to be putty in my hands as long as I played my cards right; and I planned on it. I knew she had a man, so I didn't have to spend a lot of time with her. I could take it slow; plus, Raquel and I were trying to work things out. I know a lot of guys who shit on their relationships with women, but I never set out to hurt Raquel; it just seemed to always happen that way.

One day I came back to the crib and Raquel had moved out; but get this, she left a note and $2,000. Now that's some G shit on her behalf. Me being me, I said, "Fuck it," but I knew it wasn't over between us. In her own way, she was trying to teach me a lesson. I gave her a couple of days before I tried to contact her. We were still cool. She just needed a little space to clear her mind, so I gave her that. Shit…I'm a pimp. I knew she wasn't going anywhere; at least, not yet.

I started to visit Honey at work more, and we were talking on the phone a lot; hitting it off really well. I also had five other chicks on the team that because of the breakup with Raquel, I now had more time to play with. Raquel was a female G though; she had stacked dough over the last couple of months since I was paying the bills. I knew that would happen and I owed it to her in a way, so it didn't bother me. She got her own crib; a nice little condo. I'd see her once a week or so. Most of the time it was dinner or pool and a drink; no sex though. It was time for me to work on her mind. Like an old pimp movie once said, "You can control any bitch's body, but it's her mind you need to control." Not to mention the fact that I was fucking so many bitches that it didn't matter to me that I wasn't fucking Raquel.

During this time, I was also taking trips to New York to pick up Coach bags, Prada bags, Louie Vuitton, and all types of women's stuff and I was having Honey sell them at the strip club and I would hit her off with a couple of things here and there. It was another little hustle that I was trying to add to my portfolio. I was adding a little dough to the stash even with my mom and aunt and my girl cousins hitting me off for a bag every once in a while.

Honey finally got rid of her man totally. He was a scrub anyway. She also got her own crib, so I would spend some nights over there. She had the tightest pussy. It was one of those ones you had to open up like a seashell to get to the pussy lips. I've never understood how dudes could be gay. I've always loved the female body. God knew what He was doing when He put them together.

Everything was going good for me. It seemed like things were falling in place. At least, it seemed that way. I even started to buy cars to sell. I was buying anything I could get my hands on: minivans, Audi, Impalas, Civics…everything. Raquel and I were doing well also. We were looking at houses to buy. I was on some young Don shit. I gave up my crib. I was never there anyway. I stayed at either Raquel's, Honey's, or one of my other chick's cribs. I bought Raquel a little Pit Bull puppy and we named it Juelz; even though it was a girl pup. In return, she bought me a male Pit that I named Game. I didn't adopt the saying, *Carpe Diem, seize the moment*, until years later; but it was times like this one that I wish I had seized the moment.

Shit...I was happy then, but there was always something missing because I still wasn't living fully legal. I still had to look over my shoulder all the time. In the life I was living, you could bump into anyone from your past. Someone you robbed, one of your hoes' brothers, or just anything like that. Or, I could just get caught up in a sale or something like that. I was living on the edge at that point in my life. I started to have small doubts about the game. In my head, I was making all the right decisions to leave it alone. When you are in the streets, you think about where you wanna be and where you wanna go with it, but you always know that things can change at any moment.

They say the game is played, not lived, and I was living it to the fullest at that point.

Chapter 6

A couple of months later, Raquel and I bought a two-family house. I was twenty-five, she was nineteen; we were about to become landlords and house owners at a young age. Over the next year, we both went through so many changes that neither one of us could have predicted at the time. Everything started off good. We were planning for the future, but there was one problem. I was still doing dirt. It was almost like I was living a double life. I was juggling Raquel, Honey, and escort business, dealing drugs, buying and selling cars, selling ladies clothing and accessories, and being a house owner and landlord. I had a lot on my plate. I was at the top of my game. I even got another studio apartment about six blocks away to keep my work at so that I could do my dirt. Like Biggie said, "Don't do dirt where you rest at." It was a sweet deal too. I knew the older couple who owned the building, so I paid my rent in coke.

At our house, I had plenty of parking spaces, so it was like a mini car lot. I would have at least six to ten cars there at a time. My worth was building, and then I came up even more. This chick I knew named Latasha was moving mad weight, but she was so sloppy with her hustle. Either I was going to get her, or the cops, or both. With that in mind, I started to plot on her. I would grab an ounce or so off of her every once in a while and she would show up with eight to ten ounces bagged up, showing it off like she was fresh. *You don't flaunt shit in front of a hungry nigga*; plus, it's just stupid to carry that much weight while just driving around. She was going to get got one way or another, so I didn't feel bad about what I was going to do.

She was looking for a place to stash her shit so I got her a hookup in the building where I kept my shit. The landlord didn't need any references, so she was let in with just a deposit and first month's rent. My plan was moving in motion. I knew where her shit would be, I just needed to wait until it was worth my while and she was holding a lot of work.

I had always blessed my mom on my licks, but on this one, I hooked her up a lil differently. I love my mom to death; but she was a hustler like me, and a little greedy. She loved money. She would milk the cow till it was dead though. Latasha ran with another chick and altogether, they had three kids and they always needed overnight babysitters. They would drop the kids off for three days at a time for $600 for the three days. I even had Latasha pay the three days in advance, so the first week, my mom got $1,200. Mom loved to gamble, Bingo, Lotto tickets...all that shit; so money in her hands didn't last very long. I explained to my mother that the gig wouldn't last that long because Latasha's time was going to run out. My mother made $3,800 that month just to babysit. By the end of the month, it was my time to make a move. I tried to put my boys down with it even though I could have handled it by myself.

Latasha was out of town for a couple of days and one of her biggest problems was she talked too goddamn much. She told me that she had just re-upped and that she kept the shit in the bathroom in the drop ceiling. My homeboy broke a window leading into the crib, but when he did, the building...which should have been empty that day, wasn't. So a nosey neighbor came out to check when they heard the noise. My boy tried to explain that he was Latasha's man and she had lost her keys and needed stuff out of the crib. Normally, the neighbor was at work at that time of the day, and seeing that Latasha had only lived there for a little over a month, the man didn't argue with my boy. He just went inside his apartment.

At that point, my boy was a little nervous about going in, so when he went in the crib, he rushed through. He ripped the ceiling down and searched real quick. He messed the apartment up a little, but to my surprise, he turned up nothing.

I was in shock. I know what you're thinking...*My man got me*. I thought the same thing at first, but I had known my dude for over fifteen years; he wasn't like that. So I called the dumb bitch up and told her that her crib had been broken into and that everything was flipped over and the bathroom ceiling was ripped down.

She started to cry a bit and said, "Why does this keep happening to me?"

Inside I was thinking, *Cause you sloppy, bitch.* But instead I said, "I'm going to have the landlord let me in to check on things, tell me where you had your stash and I'll check on it for you."

She told me some was in the bathroom ceiling and there was some more in the bottom of a lamp. I called the landlord and explained the situation and told him that I'd hook him up just to let me in. He and his wife were coke heads, so I promised him a phat bag if he opened the door.

"No problem," he said.

I had him wait outside of his own building; now that's some gangster shit. I just didn't need him looking over my shoulder in case I found a lot stashed in the house. When I went in, I was able to take my time. First I went into the bathroom. I placed my hand in the tiles of the ceiling that was left, searching left to right. I didn't find anything.

"Damn, my man got me," I said, but then I got on my tippy toes and reached in a little further and I felt a bag. I grabbed it and it was all crack. It looked like a couple of ounces. I put it in my pocket and went straight to the lamp. I peeled the bottom of it off and BANG...another bag with about the same amount in it, but it was some yellow, raw, fish scale coke. I placed the bag in my pocket too and I went outside. I told the landlord that I found some shit, but that it was all crack. He didn't smoke; he was a sniffer, so I told him once I found out what I had, I'd hook him up. He didn't ask any questons and I was on my way out.

I couldn't wait to get to my house to see what I had. I didn't want to leave the shit in my spot downstairs from hers just in case something happened, so I drove toward my house a couple of blocks away. I wasn't going to leave it in the house that Raquel and I lived in. I happened to be fucking the chubby girl that lived next door, so I went to her crib. I knew it was safe there; and besides, she had kids and needed to go school shopping for them and could use a couple hundred dollars.

I know what you're thinking...*How much was it?* Well, the bag of crack weighted about 115 grams, 4 ounces; and the fish scale coke weighed about to 120 grams . So for you none drug dealers, that's a little over a half pound of coke and I didn't have to split it with anyone, so it was going to be all profit. I was going to sell it at $100 a gram, so you do the math. I kept my word. I gave the landlord ten grams; well seven grams, but after I threw three grams of cut on it, it was ten grams. So that left me with 228 grams. I was going to be good for a hot minute.

Even though my money was doing well, Raquel and I weren't. It had been about a year since we bought the house and I never stopped cheating like I had planned to. I was still fucking Honey, a chick named Danielle, the next door neighbor chick, and a couple of others. *Yeah...I was a dog.* Raquel was growing into a woman and she wasn't the little girl I had met who was going to keep putting up with my shit. I don't blame her.

At that point, we were sleeping in separate rooms and there was mad tension in the house. She decided to move out and move to her mother's house. She wasn't even gone twenty-four hours and Danielle, who I had been fucking for about a year, came over with her girl. Danielle was a fucking freak. She was nineteen, about 100 pounds, and had nice little tits. She was an ex cheerleader, so she was flexible as shit. She was always hanging with sluts just like her. I ended up fucking so many of her friends that I lost count. The chick she brought over was twenty-two, blond, and about 115 pounds and she had big titties. She had a baby, but you couldn't tell it. She had a bad ass body on her even though she had just had her kid two years ago. She was still producing milk. She could squirt breast milk across the room. I don't know about you...but that shit turned me on. When they came over, it was on. We all fucked for the next two days...freaky ass bitches.

As you can see, Raquel leaving didn't affect me; at least, not right away. Man...if the walls could speak. The shit I did in that crib over the next couple of months was epic. Pussy was falling out the sky. Another chick that I hadn't fucked yet named Jen, who would come by and smoke blunts, came by a couple of nights later; while she was there, Danielle's friend, Carissa called looking to also smoke. Carissa was bad. She looked like the singer, Rihanna. No lie. Same short cut and everything, she just had bigger titties.

We started sipping and smoking and both chicks were hitting it off. I hadn't fucked Carissa yet either at the time. I don't know if it was the Hennessy in me, or my pimping, or what…but I just simply said, "Let's all just get naked and go in the other room."

With no hesitation, Carissa said, "Ok" and she started walking to the bedroom and Jen followed. I looked up to the sky and thanked God for another threesome in less than a week. Like I said, *pussy was falling from the sky*. I went in those bitches raw dog…busting nuts in both of them. With two different pussies to choose from, I wanted to feel the difference…you dig?

I was on a roll. I was loving the single life. It's like bitches know when you're single. They can smell that shit; especially freaks. Now the best sex that I have had to this day came from a red head chick named Farrah. She told me that the only way she could cum was by being fucked in her ass.

You gotta love that.

She did everything right; she would ride the dick and just pull it out and put it in her ass. She moaned like a fucking porn star. She sucked dick like one too. After you would cum, she would do this thing where she would bend over like you were hitting it from the back, and with her face on the bed, she would take her right hand with her fingers in the West Side Connection gang symbol, and with the two fingers in the middle, she would stick them in her ass. Then with her left hand, she would put her fingers in between her legs and play with her pussy; it was priceless. She was a fucking freak. In the words of a White boy...*it was awesome!*

My freak feast didn't end there. That same month, I threw a party. Roy Jones Jr. was fighting Trinadad. I had Danielle and one of her girls do a girl-on-girl show and charged $50 a head. I had my mom make 400 chicken wings, some potato salad and Spanish rice. There was a full bar with my Asian homegirl as the bartender and two kegs; Budweiser in one and Heineken in the other. And yes…I fucked Danielle's friend. I can't remember what the bitch's name was, but she had a phat ass…I remember that much. It was a hell of a party. I got so much pussy that year that I am lucky my dick didn't fall off.

I was still kicking it with Honey, and the house was Raquel's name. I was on the deed and title, so I had no worries. I met with Raquel at least once a month to give her the money for the mortgage. I started to slow down with all the hoes and got more serious with Honey and spent some time with Raquel. I'd spend a couple of nights with Honey and a couple with Raquel. I juggled both of them without any troubles; it was going smooth.

I knew sooner or later it was going to go up in flames even I was surprised it had lasted so long. Then one day, Raquel was at the house during the day. We had sex and I gave her the money for the mortgage and she went on her way. I had plans with Honey to come to the crib and spend the night. She picked me up at the house and we went to go get some movies and Chinese food.

Honey knew about Raquel and I owning the house together. I had told her our relationship was over though and that we didn't get along. I told her that I would see her to give her the mortgage money and that was it. That was a lie.

Well, the tenants that we had living upstairs had moved out. I did not know that Raquel was going to come back that night to paint, so when Honey and I pulled up and Raquel was on the porch smoking a cigarette, I was surprised to see her.

Errr...pump your brakes! I hate to stop the book like this...but like I said, I'm in jail writing this and you won't believe what just happened. I'll get back to that other shit later.

*****

I get called down to booking and there's a sheriff there to serve me papers. This punk ass bitch Raquel is trying to get my name off the deed and title. She has gotten a lawyer and is trying to play me, saying I never put any money into the house; just a punk ass $250. Are you serious? I am easily $40,000 into the house. Yes...I haven't given her shit in the last couple of years, but that's for all kinds of different reasons that I'll explain later. She has me looking like a pimp and shit…which you know how I do by now. She is saying that I persuaded her to put my name on that shit. Well, maybe I did a little, but for her to say I've only put $250 in it over the last seven years…that bitch is out of her fucking mind.

I feel bad about all the dirt and drama that I put her through, but I'm not going to let her play me on this shit. Like R. Kelly said, "A woman scorned."

*****

Now where was I? Ok…so back to when I pulled up to the house with Honey and Raquel was on the porch. Like I said, I was surprised, but you know I played it like a pimp. I looked at Honey all serious and shit and said, "What the fuck is this bitch doing here disrespecting my privacy and shit? I haven't even spoken to her."

That's what I said, knowing damn well I fucked her and gave her money a couple of hours before that. I felt bad for what I was about to say to Raquel because we were being cool and all, but I looked at it like it was her fault for not calling first. I told Honey to pull to the end of the parking lot. I did not need those two bitches talking. That shit would have blown up right in my face real quick.

I said to Honey, "Wait in the car while I get rid of this bitch," all mad and shit while trying to keep my cool like a pimp should. I stormed up to Raquel with my hands waiving around so Honey could see me from the rear view mirror, but I kept my voice low just in case she had opened the window trying to listen which I knew she was going to do.

"What the fuck are you doing here," I said to Raquel.

"Well, I was painting upstairs," she replied.

"Oh, you don't have to call? What about my fucking privacy?"

She wasn't hearing that shit. She shouted back, "Who is that bitch!"

"A friend, but that's none of your business anyway."

She came back with, "Well, if it's a friend...introduce me."

She was right, but Raquel and I weren't together, so I didn't feel like I owed her any explanations so I shot that down real quick. Besides, it was a lie and that would have been crazy to do on my part. Within seconds, they would have realized I was juggling them both for the last two years. Those bitches would have killed me.

I could see the hurt in Raquel's face seeing as though she had hoped for us to work things out. I also saw the hate in her face that things would never be the same between us again. I knew that moment was going to be the last time she let her guard down and let me hurt her no matter how much she loved me.

Before she could say anything, I walked back toward the car and told Honey, "This bitch is fucking crazy. I'm not going to stay here tonight. Meet me down the street at the bar while I grab my shit and I'll meet you there in a couple of minutes."

I walked back toward Raquel and when Honey drove by to leave, the looks that those two bitches gave each other were deadly. I told Raquel that she was fucked up for not calling first and then I went into the house to grab some clothes for the night. I hated treating Raquel like that, but like I had told her before, "All the shit I put you through will only put you on point for the next relationship that you're in."

I know that sounds fucked up, but it was the truth. I left that night and knew shit was all fucked up on the real. I was tired of living in that house anyway.

I met up with Honey at the bar and started to turn my mack up on her. We were spending mad time together anyway, so I had made up my mind just to move into her crib. It wasn't the best decision that I ever made, but I needed to make some changes anyway. I was always a good decision maker in the moment of something, but sometimes I wish that I slowed down and thought things through more when my mind was clear.

Within a couple of days, most of my shit was moved into Honey's place; all the rest I could sell. I was a hood nigga, so all I needed was six pairs of new kicks, some jeans, jogging pants, and a dozen white and black tees. I was getting calls from Raquel, but I could tell there was no turning back. That bitch wanted me out of the house. She had no idea that I was already out, so when she started yelling and bitching me out, thinking I was gonna try to stay, I cussed her ass out and let her know that I was already on to something different. That wasn't the best move because she just got angrier and over the next week, she just went even harder on the phone with me.

She was taught by the best. I couldn't even argue with her. She was using all the sayings that I would usually say and she was saying them first. Maybe I had taught her to well. She was talking in the third person. This bitch had gone crazy. I knew it was over. She cut off all the love for me. In a way, I didn't blame her and I wasn't mad. Shit...I had Honey. Honey was bad. She was all tanned up, long, black hair, a pretty face and a bad ass body. With her stripping, she was bringing in $3,000 a week just working a couple of days. I'm not going to lie...it was fun fucking both of them. They had totally different pussies. Honey's...I would call my seashell; it was one of those pussies that you had to open to get to the lips and when you did, you had to play with the clit to get it wet and she was so tight it was crazy. Raquel had the nicest pussy lips that just needed to be touched once and she got so wet it was also crazy. I had the best of both worlds. I'm not complaining though; it was fun while it lasted. All good things have to come to an end sooner or later.

Now living with Honey was all peaches and cream at first. Just like I have found out many times before, once you live with a girl, you get to see all the things you had never noticed about them before. At first, things were so good that I was making long time plans with her; talking about driving cross country and having her do amateur nights in every state for extra dough for our trip! We were both saving dough, and the sex was great. With the stripper hours that she had, I had most days to myself. She slept during the day like most strippers do, and she worked at night until 3:00 am. When she got home, we would smoke a blunt and head to an all-night gym. We would work out, then go for breakfast and then come back and fuck till we both passed out. But at that point, I stopped drinking and started to notice little things about her.

First, the bitch was bipolar; which most bitches are, but with her being a stripper, it made it even worse. She would wake up like nothing ever happened. It was a roller coaster with that bitch. As good looking as she was, it made her ugly. Then she stopped cleaning. It wasn't too bad because we would have my Aunt come in twice a week and do laundry and clean for $100, but her being bipolar made me not want to fuck her anymore.

Over the next couple of months, it got worse and the sex was less and less, and the relationship started to fuck with my money making. She would chip in, but she was smoking all the smoke up and the days that we ran out…she was even worse until I re-upped. It seemed like the more we bought, the more she smoked. I was trying to cut back, so my temper was even shorter. That bitch was driving me crazy.

It got to the point where I loved when she was asleep or at work. I needed to make some moves, so I started to look for a different crib during the day while she was at work. One day after about three or four months of living with her, the bitch came home after running her errands and she was in rare form, screaming and yelling about everything. I couldn't take it anymore. I hadn't found a crib yet, but I didn't care. I made up my mind that I was going to move out while she was at work and stay with my mother until I found a crib. I didn't want to be there when she got home. The bitch was crazy and I didn't know what she would have done if we had to talk about it. I just knew someone would have ended up in jail and it wasn't going to be my black ass.

I wish I could have seen her face when all my shit was gone. She was so bad that no dude had ever left her ass. Shit…every guy that went into that strip club would have put up with anything to be with her. But when I thought about it, I said to myself, "Fuck it. I'm a pimp. Bitches come and go. I've never had a problem fucking dimes, strippers, or bad bitches!"

So I moved out that night and went to Ma Dukes' crib. That bitch blew up my phone, but I was asleep and I had it on silent. That bitch called my mom's house at 2:00 am asking for me. My mom had always been a G, and even though she always liked

Honey, she said coldly when she answered the phone, "Do you know what time it is? He is sleeping," and then she hung up. My mom always had my back when I made decisions about bitches.

I found a crib two days later and I waited a week to return Honey's calls. We were cool and she kind of understood, so we kept it cool for a little while. Raquel and I spoke a little because of the house, but shit was different at that point for me. A new crib for me, but I was the same nigga.

Chapter 7

I started to fuck all types of bitches; Black, White, Spanish, and Asian. Over the next couple of months, so many hoes came and went. I made money off of a few of them and fucked the rest, but at that point, my patience was thin. If a bitch got on my nerves, she was cut real quickly I was kicking them out like martin. I didn't care if they were bringing me dough or not. I lost a lot of good bitches because of my attitude, but I didn't give a fuck. There was always one to replace them. I couldn't click with any of the bitches. My mind was in other places. Over the years, I would still have dreams about Channa. She was the only girl I had ever loved.

I used to have this one dream all the time that we were laying in the bed facing each other and I was looking in her eyes explaining that I would always love her no matter what. I told her that she would always have a place in my heart even if we were young when we had our relationship and couldn't be together. The dream was so real. I would always wake up in cold sweats and be mad at myself that I was still thinking about her. I knew I needed closure to stop the dreams. So much time had passed, I knew we couldn't be together. Shit…I hadn't changed. I was still a pimp and a drug dealer and that was the main reason we broke up. I couldn't leave the life and I definitely couldn't keep my dick in my pants. Shit…I had the same dream while sleeping next to any bitch I ever lived with. Shit…even in my dreams, I was cheating on the bitches I was with, so I knew it would never work, but something in me still wanted to see her even if it was just for a night of fun. *But I was a pimp, playa ass nigga; what was I even doing thinking about any one bitch?* So I put that playa ass shit to the back of my mind and went on with my life.

I started to notice things around me were changing. I was getting older. People that I ran with were changing their life. My cousin, Galen, left the game and had a son. I was happy for him. I just knew he would make a good father. Shit…neither one of us ever had one in our lives, so I knew he wouldn't do that to his son, even if he wasn't with the chick. I was right. He took the money he had and opened a personal training studio and as soon as his son could walk, he had a baseball, basketball and football in his hand. Galen was gonna teach his son everything he knew about sports and his son was learning from the best. To this day, I think Galen was the best athlete I have ever seen play. He could have gone pro in any sport if he didn't blow out his knee; and with the way he was able to put the street life behind him, I had to be proud of my cousin.

People around me were starting to grow up. One of my connects – Tony from back in the day – was on the same path. He became a manager of a high-class restaurant in Boston's South End, which I knew he owned a little stock in the restaurant, and to my surprise, he got married. He had been a playa like me.

He could have been a pimp, but he always said, "That's not a white man's game. I'll leave that up to the brothers."

Tony always spoke the truth. I had mad respect for him. He also was able to put the street life behind him. At least that's what I think I always thought he had…connection to the mafia, but he would always deny it; which the mafia was known for doing, so I'm not sure about the truth of that.

The biggest shock of everything that was going on around me was the person that I had the most respect for and wanted more than anything to be like…well, one of them…was my uncle. My uncle was the man in my life growing up that was my real first look into the game of pimping and the lifestyle it carried. I remember it was 1988, I was ten and he had a silver '88, 318 BMW with black leather seats. He picked me up and took me for a ride. He told me to buckle up and he got on the highway and punched it…sunroof open, sun shining on my nappy head; it was heaven.

My uncle wore a cool gold nugget pinky ring with a diamond in the upper right corner, with a matching nugget bracelet. On the other hand he had a big gold lion face ring. He always wore a gold chain, and a gold earring. He never left the crib without two pagers and a knot of cash in both pockets. He was living the high life, is what I thought.

He would always say, "Do the right thing. Stay in school. Don't do drugs and don't be like me; it's not the way to live."

Now that's hard for a young black kid to understand because to me, it looked like this way of life was the way to live. We raced his shiny new cars on the highway. My uncle stayed around fly white females. We pulled up on this house and a white girl with daisy duke shorts, a half shirt, high heels and blond hair came out. She was hot. I couldn't keep my eyes off of her. I went to jump out of the front seat to give it to her, but my uncle grabbed my shoulder.

"Stay there."

He looked at the chick and said, "Bitch, get in the back."

I felt like the man. First, because of the power my uncle had; and second, shit...adults always sat up front.

When we drove off, I had even more respect for my uncle if that was even possible. I thought to myself, Damn, when I have nephews, I'm gonna have it like that.

That feeling was amazing. Shit…if my uncle was a lawyer grabbing his secretary, that is what I would have seen, but that wasn't the case. I wanted the power. I wanted the BMW. I wanted the money. I wanted the gold. I wanted all that shit and more. It made my hunger grow even more for the lifestyle. Damn, how do you show a kid all that and then tell him that he don't want to live like that? It wouldn't be too many years later till I would understand what he was trying to do for me; but at that point, it was too late and I was too deep in the game. But to this day, I respect my Uncle Mando for he's a real G in my book; literally!!!

My uncle ended up getting caught on a charge for fucking with this chick that I am pretty sure another pimp had set him up. He ended up spending five years in jail, and when he came out, he found God. He wifed up one of the first chicks he got with when he got out and had two kids of his own. He didn't stay with the chick, but he took both of his boys from her and became a single father, also leaving the street life and pimp game behind him; he was as straight as an arrow. He could always sing, so he started a karaoke business and got a couple of jobs at Chinese restaurants all over New England making $200 a night. It wasn't the money he used to get, but he didn't have to look over his shoulder; so he, too, had changed his life for the better.

Now the man I wanted most to be like was the pimp nigga, Shane. What happened to him, no one could have predicted. First off, he didn't drink or do drugs, but I guess from all the stress that came with the pimp game and genetics, he had high blood pressure, which was a shock to me because I never really saw him lose his cool. But one day while he was working out, he collapsed off the tread mill and was rushed to the hospital. He had a brain hemorrhage. He had stopped taking his blood pressure medicine and his body went into shock. When he arrived at the hospital he was in a coma. they operated on his brain and took a chunk out. They said he would never walk again and would be lucky to come out of the coma.

The doctors were wrong. He came out of the coma, but the left side of his body was paralyzed and his speech was slurred. He was never going to be the same. All but one of his girls left him and he had had like thirteen at the time. He had to sell his two houses and lost all the cars. It took him over a year to even be able to walk again, which the doctors had said he would never be able to do. They didn't know he was a pimp tho. He was damn near broke. A lot of people said it was karma for all the dirt that he had done over the years.

I was thirty when all of that happened and I tried to take it all in. I started to have doubts about the life I had lead for the last twenty years. I wanted to slow down and take my life in a different direction, but what was I going to do? I was a pimp and a drug dealer. That's what I knew. I hadn't had a legal job in over a decade. My money was pretty low. I owned a Jaguar S-Type, a BMW 540, a Yukon, and a couple of cheaper cars. My stash was at an all-time low. If I was lucky, I could liquidate and get like $35,000…and that was only if I was lucky. I owned the house with Raquel, but the market was all fucked up.

I needed to make some moves, but truth be told, I wasn't the nigga I was when I was twenty-one. At twenty-one, I had no fear; or at least I was just too young to think about it. But at thirty, I thought about everything. I wasn't sure what my next move was going to be. I was still having dreams about Channa. I had heard that she had just had a baby. The same goes for Honey. She had one also. What the fuck was going on? Everyone was doing things and I was doing the same old shit. I was fucking like six different bitches, but they did nothing for me. I decided I needed to go out for a little while to get my mind right, so I went to a local bar in Nashua called Boston Billiards. I hadn't been there in a while. Everything happens for a reason, was always my saying and that night it proved to be just that way.

I had only been there for ten minutes when I got a tap on my shoulder and it was Channa's brother. They were only a couple years apart in age. He and I always got along. I bought him a couple of beers and we talked for a long time. He told me that out of all of Channa's boyfriends, he had always like me the most. It had been ten years since she and I had been together. I explained to him that I would always love his sister and that she would always have a special place in my heart. I also told him that at least once a year, sometimes more, I had dreams about her. It was like she was haunting me in my dreams.

We both laughed and drank. He knew his sister had a crazy effect on guys, but he also knew I wasn't anything like those punks. I was a pimp and a gangster ass nigga. Shit…he once came on a lick with me, so he knew how I used to get down. Like I said, he always liked me, so he told me that Channa was single and that she worked in this little bar in Dracut, Mass, where she had worked a little when we were dating. He told me I should go there to see her. I was doubtful. I was never that type of dude, not only had it been ten years, but I was always the type that when it's over, it's over. Shit…I'm no stalker.

We both left the bar drunk as a skunk. I hugged him goodbye and told him that I would think about it. I went home that night and called up one of my freaky ass hoes to help me go to sleep. I woke up the next day with a half-naked stripper next to me with a lot on my mind. I knew the bitch wasn't going to get up until 2:00 in the afternoon. Even though we were up till 6:00 am, I woke up at 10:30 am. I couldn't sleep, so I went to the gym to clear my mind. While I was running, doing my cardio…a lot went through my mind. Channa had just had a kid; her daughter was beautiful and not even one year old yet, so even though she wasn't with the baby's daddy, I knew he was still around. That meant that I also knew things would never be the same as it was when we were young and in love. But I didn't care. I just wanted a little closure.

When we broke up, one of the main reasons was that I was young and dumb and in the street life hard. Much had not changed. I was older and smarter, but I was still doing the same shit. I knew it couldn't work between us, but it was worth the try just to have some fun. I had made up my mind that I was going to visit her at work. Her brother had given me her work hours and I picked the slowest day…Monday, to go there. I decided to show up early so as not to come during the lunch rush so that I would have a little time to talk to her. When Monday came, I was nervous, as if I were thirteen years old or something. For that whole week, I had planned what I would say to her. My mind was going back and forth with the possibilities of what if she didn't want to talk. What if we hit it off again. Man…my mind was going crazy.

I had gone out and bought brand new Jordan 4s – my favorite, black on black, and a new black champion sweat suit. I went lite on the bling; just platinum studs in my ears and a silver Armani Exchange watch on my left wrist. I got a fresh bald cut with my face all lined up. I even got the Jag S-Type cleaned; all shined up with enough armorall on the tires and leather seats that I was slipping and sliding everywhere.

I arrived at the bar at 11:30 am; they were already open. I parked out front, just thinking and bumping some Max B. I'm not going to front; like Mobb Deep said, "I was a shook one." I had to hype myself up before I walked into the bar. I sprayed a final couple of sprays of some Dolce & Gabbana. It would help jog her memories. I used to wear it when we were dating. I got some more especially for the meeting. I hadn't worn it in years.

My palms were sweating as I entered the bar. Her back was toward me while she made someone a drink. I could tell it was her by her long black hair and those hips. My heart was beating a mile a minute, but I was going to keep my cool. *Shit...I'm a pimp*, I thought before I sat down. When she turned around, she paused...and then she spoke my government name in full. I could tell she was in shock. I smiled with a cool, but happy look on my face. As much as I was happy to see her, my pimping jumped in to full affect. I hadn't drank in about eight months; which I would do every once in a while to clean my system, so I just ordered water.

My mouth game was always on point, so the convo went smooth. I explained to her that I had bumped into her brother a week ago and we were talking and he told me she still worked there a couple of days a week, so I wanted to drop in and say hi. It seemed as if she did not mind that I had stopped by, but it seemed to throw her off a bit when I asked if I could call her and take her out for a drink or something. Her expression did not show that she was thrown off by my invitation, so I don't think that is what took her off guard. I think what got her was when she went to reach for a pen to write her phone number down and I rattled it off quick. I think that is what startled her. Little did she know that I had not only used her number ten years ago, but I had also called it a couple of times when I had those dreams and woke up in a cold sweat. I had tried the number several times over the years and once I heard her voice on the other end, I didn't have enough balls to speak and leave a message.

"Wow, you still remember my number?" she asked.

"I remember a lot about you," I replied with a wink.

She told me that they were getting ready to start to have their lunch rush and I took that as a sign to leave. I told her that it was nice seeing her and that I would text her and then I left. At first, I thought she had acted a little strange at the end, but I just chalked it up as she was caught off guard by my presence. I was right. I later found out that she had called her brother to see if he had my number because she felt weird about how the conversation ended and hoped that I was going to call her and had not taken things the wrong way.

I felt like a little ass kid. I sent her a text within fifteen minutes from me leaving her job. I told her that it was nice to see her face and hear her voice after all the time that had passed. I also told her it would be nice to go out for a drink, but if she didn't want to go, that was ok...I understood. She told me she would love to go out for a drink in a couple of days. Again...I felt like a fat kid with a piece of cake, like Fifty Cents says in his song. Shit...I was floating on cloud nine. I didn't know what to think.

Was I going to get closure, or was this my destiny falling into play after all this time. If you let it go and it comes back, it's meant to be, ran through my mind, but deep down, I just wanted some closure; a wild night in the sack...if you feel me.

Over the next couple of months, shit couldn't have gone any better. The first date was a hit. Shit...we started to talk on the phone like kids for hours just like when we were twenty-one. She hadn't had sex in over eight months, so I knew that was a sign by the second date. I rented a hotel near her house where she had moved in with her daddy to keep him company since his wife's death and the breakup she had with her baby's daddy. Her father helped baby sit when she worked. I went to the store and grabbed CDs of all the old slow jams that we used to fuck to when they were on tape. Jon B's *Cool Relax* album was the shit. Donnel Jones, Case, Craig David, R. Kelly...shit...the list goes on. I grabbed some chocolate covered strawberries, a bottle of Dom P. and some scented candles. I was gonna get that ass after all that time. Shit...you can't say no to a pimp when he is making all the right moves; and of course, she couldn't.

We fucked all night; well, at least till 4:00 am. She had to get back to her daughter before her dad woke up for work. I was in fucking heaven. What's strange is the dream that I had had so many times came true more than once over the next couple of months. I found myself lying in a bed looking her eye to eye telling her how much I missed her and that I would always love her. It was like déjà vu.

I couldn't believe the way I was feeling. At least once or twice a week, I was renting a hotel so that we could fuck and spend some time together. I was starting to feel like a cheap prostitute. We would bang and she would leave at 4:00 in the morning. Any other chick, I wouldn't have cared; but with her, I needed to tell myself, *Fuck it. I'm getting the closure that I wanted and having fun at the same time.* Some nights, I'd leave after she did. Damn...if I was going to sleep alone, I'd do it at my own crib. Some nights, I'd call up a stripper chick because I knew she would be up plus I would still have another round or two in me, and I was trying to cover up my feelings. Luv is strange. That shit can make a grown man cry like a baby and do some punk-ass shit.

I was a pimp though, so I always handled my feelings in a different way and fucking two dime pieces in a night was one of them. To this day, I have never been broke up with...or left behind. I am the one that does the breaking up before it happens.

To me, I've been lucky with that my whole life. Even with Channa, I broke up with her and even though I thought about her, I never let it get the best of me; at least not until ten years later.

The hotel shit was getting a little old. Over the years, I've spent tons of nights in hotels, so I decided to move from Manchester to Nashua so that she didn't have to drive so far and it would give us more time to spend with each other. I knew things could never be how they were when we were kids; damn…she had a kid of her own now, but I was going to ride the wave for as long as possible.

Channa and I had lunch with my mother a couple of times since my mom hadn't seen Channa in years and she knew how I felt about her. Things were going good. A couple of nights, I even snuck in her daddy's crib while he was sleeping to spend the night with her. I was feeling like a little kid again. She wasn't stupid though…shit, I wasn't working, but had money and a couple of whips. The Jag S-Type alone was a standout car. I had sold the BMW 540 and the Yukon and got a Jeep that was sitting on 24's. I told her that I was selling cars and saved a lot of money when I was doing that, and that's what I was living on. I wouldn't make any moves around her. When I spent time with her it was all about her.

She had stopped her whole life over the last couple of months spending all her free time with me. I knew eventually she would have to resume her life again. I also had a planned vacation set up with my cousin, Ciara. We were going on a cruise to Jamaica and I had to meet her in Miami. I had so much on my mind and I didn't want to leave Channa. I needed more time to put my Mack down, but I also couldn't disappoint my cousin. We had had the vacation planned for almost a year. Well, at least my cousin did. She had bought me the cruise ticket for my birthday. She was always on point with shit like that. Damn, I got my plane ticket to Miami a couple of weeks before our vacation and my cousin had to remind me. I always did things last minute. So when it was time to head out for my vacation, Channa and I spent the night before it together and she was going to come back the next day and take me to the

Airport since she had business out that way. After Channa left that night, I had a freaky bitch named Becca come over. Shit...I still felt like a cheap hoe every time Channa left me after sex. I always needed some more ass to get over my feelings once she was gone. Becca was good at that. She would take it in the ass like a champ and then suck the shit off my dick. She was an eight; mixed with Black and White. She had a bad body, a pretty face and one of those short haircuts, but she pulled it off. I always say that a girl has to have a real pretty face to pull off one of those short haircuts and Becca did that well. I couldn't even remember the last time I had fucked her in the pussy; it was almost always up the ass. She was a freak like that. To this day I still love a down ass dirty freak.

The next morning, Channa showed up to take me to the airport. She drove a silver Benz. While she was driving, I would just look at her. She was so damn fine. I had gotten my closure, but I knew if things between us were to go any further, when I came back from vacation, I was going to have to make some major moves and changes in my life. I kissed Channa on the cheek and got on the plane to Miami.

Chapter 8

My cousin and I got to the airport in Miami at the same time. I love my cousin dearly; she is so damn cool. We had always talked about making shirts that said, "She is my Cousin" and "He is my Cousin" because people were always getting the wrong idea when we were together. We are both good looking and when we are together, we are always so happy that people mistake us for a couple.

When Ciara got off the plane she said she had something for me. When we got to the hotel, to my surprise, she had gotten the T-shirts made; she was always so thoughtful like that. We hit the liquor store and got some bottles for the night and some for the cruise. We spent two nights in Miami hitting the clubs at night and sleeping all day. At the club, we worked like a team; if I noticed a guy checking her out, if she thought he was cute, I'd approach him, explain that she was my cousin and the next thing you know, the fool would be buying both of our drinks. What he didn't know was my cousin wasn't easy; shit…to this day she is thirty-five years old and has only had sex with four guys. I can't say that about many girls I know. The game we played in the club worked both ways, if I noticed a female and got that eye contact, Ciara would approach them and explain that I was her cousin and tell them how good of a guy I was. It always worked. We made a good team.

After two days in Miami, we boarded the boat for Jamaica. We took a seven day cruise. We did everything that week: massages, swimming with dolphins, gambling, clubs, jet skis, and we even rented mopeds on the island. We had a good time. I met some bad ass Cuban bitches.

I kept in touch with Channa during that week. I also got a call from my boy that lived across the street from my crib. The dumb ass bitch, Becca tried to break in my crib thinking that maybe I left some drugs in there. She tried to jimmy the lock with her debit card and it fell through the slot in the door and landed on the other side. Then the dumb ass went downstairs to the landlord that owned a restaurant underneath my crib. She told the owner that I wanted her to grab something for me. He knew I was on vacation and thought it was strange so he contacted my boy, who contacted me. My boy asked if I wanted him to check the crib. I had known him for twenty years; he was one of a couple of people that I trusted and I didn't trust a lot of people. I told him that I did want him to check my crib out and to have the landlord let him in. When he got inside, he found Becca's debit card with her name on it. I had to laugh at it even though it sucked to hear on my vacation. I had known Becca for years. Other than being a dirty freak, I knew she loved to get high, so I wasn't mad. Nothing was gone and I was going to make her butt hole pay for it when I got back; especially if she wanted her debit card back. I knew she would deny it and make up some dumb lie, but I'd deal with that when I got home. It kind of made my dick hard thinking about how dirty I was gonna treat her and that butt hole of hers. I had a night of fun to look forward to when I got home.

My cousin and I had a blast on the cruise, but I couldn't stop thinking about Channa's ass. We left Jamaica and spent another couple of days in Miami. We left Miami on the same day with me boarding my plane first. I told my cousin I would call her when I got back. I had a lot to think about on the plane ride home, like what I was going to do to separate me from the street life. The night I got home, I picked up some work: an ounce or two of coke and an ounce of weed for the head…to smoke. Even though I was in Jamaica for a week, I didn't smoke the whole time I was there. Shit…with my luck, I would have gotten caught with it and been in some island jail. I wasn't going to take the chance.

The first night, I sat, sipped on some Henny and smoked a fat blunt all by myself. I once read a book by a pimp that said that a pimp's best company is his own, and he was right. I sat and thought about my next move. I was going to open a store; an urban clothing store which I had always wanted to do and it was something legal for me to get into. The next night, I tore Becca's butt whole wide open. That also helped clear my mind. After that, I planned on waking up after I kicked that punk bitch out and start my plan of opening a store. To this day, if I put my mind to it, I can make things happen.

Two days after returning from vacation, I was putting things in action. I had already moved the two ounces of coke, so I had like $4,000 to fuck with to make things happen. I grabbed some pills to sell and started to look for a spot for the store. Within a day, I found a spot that I liked. It was in Nashua on Canal Street; a busy street that was near the hood or what could be called the hood for New Hampshire. It was in the French Hill area. I set up an appointment with the landlord to see the spot and maybe sign a lease. It was $2,000 to move in which wasn't bad. Rent was $1,000 a month. I was still talking to Channa, but things had died down. I figured that after I got the Biz up and running, maybe she would see that I was moving in the right way and that would help our relationship.

I signed the lease to the spot and was ready to make things happen. First, I went online and found display cases for the store. I wasn't sure what I was going to name the place yet, but I had time. My plan was to have a soft opening in two weeks from the time I had signed the least, which was kind of quick, but I wanted to make things happen. There were a couple of stores like the one I was going to open about twenty minutes north of me in Manchester. I knew both of the owners. When I was at the top of my drug dealing and when I came up on licks, I would go in their stores and drop a G or two on gear and tell them I wanted a store like theirs, and now I was going to have it.

I bought some shit from each store. Things that they had on discount racks and was willing to give me for a low price. It was old shit in their store, but it would be new in my store. I bought tees, kicks, mixed CDs, hats, chains, all that shit that a hood nigga would like to rock. I was making it happen. I was happy as shit. I even called Raquel's punk ass to tell her. To my surprise – which I don't know why I was surprised – she gave me an attitude and said, "So?!" I guess I deserved it. We still were not that cool even though we still had the house, but I just thought she would be happy for me seeing that on my many drunken nights, I would talk about doing something like this. The next day she called to apologize, which was cool, but it didn't matter. I was gonna make this happen one way or another. One of the guys that owned one of the urban stores, his name was Jaime, had named his store Urban Zone. He was a Mexican guy with a couple of kids and a wife. We had spent time in his store drinking beers and shooting the shit. There were many times when I'd get new bitches and I would bring them by his store to show them off to his married ass. I had known him since he had opened his store six years ago. I had spent thousands of dollars with him. I thought we were friends, but as I would later find out, there's no such thing as friends when it comes to business. I thought I could count on him for help seeing that I was twenty minutes away and not really any competition; plus, I could send business his way, but I guess he never really saw it that way. He would do little things, but he was always strange about it. Since I was not trying to treat the business like a drug game, I didn't notice all the signs at first. I'll tell you this, I wish I would have went into Biz like I ran the streets because there's no Luv in business at all. Business is dirtier than the street game and pimp game will ever be.

There was a lot I needed to learn. I still had to handle my Biz, so I wasn't going to let anything hold me back. Little by little, I was getting the store ready for the soft opening. My money was short, but I figured I would still pimp a bit till I got it up and running. What happened next would change everything I was planning. Two weeks had gone by and I had my mom and little bro at the store. I took the newspaper off the windows. I was open, but a White boy that I had known for a couple of years had been calling me to grab the last of the pills I had. I had to meet him about half an hour away from where the store was. I grabbed my mom's keys cause I never made moves in the Jag and that's what I was driving on that day. In the moment, you don't think about everything until it's too late.

I met up with the White boy at a Burger King and made the play. I thought he was acting strange, but I had been so busy that day that I was stressed out. When I went to drive away, I was surrounded by cops. There was a short chase. I had nowhere to go. I was fucked! So many things went through my mind. *Was I set up? Had the cops been watching Burger King? What was going on?* I got arrested. The cops tried to play it off, so that I wouldn't be aware that the White boy had a wire on him.

The day I opened my store, I caught a charge for a controlled drug. *What type of luck is that?* I couldn't believe it. I had opened the store, so shit like this wasn't supposed to happen. Like an old G told me once, *It's always the last move.* My head was all fucked up. I got bailed out the same night. It killed me to have to call my mom and tell her to close down the store and come and pick me up.

I really didn't know what my next move was going to be. All the fight was taken out of me. I didn't want to pimp. Over the next year, I went through so many emotions it was crazy. I wasn't sure if they were still watching me, so I stopped everything. I sold everything I had to in order to be able to pay for lawyer fees and to supply the store. The Jag was gone. The jeep was gone. The big screens, leather couches, and the jewels, everything…My savings was already tied up in the store. I was backed into a corner.

I sat in the store for hours every day wondering what God was trying to tell me. I needed so much stuff for the store to run right. I didn't have money for marketing or other important things. I needed to make the best out of the situation. I was banging bitches in the back of the store every chance I got just to take my mind off of things. I had named the store Handle Ur Biz because shortly after I signed the lease, one of the bitches I had known for years told me, "Damn, you always Handle Ur Biz" and she was right. The name just clicked and I used it for the store name. As I thought about that, I realized it was time for me to do just that.

Chapter 9

My lawyer had worked out a plea deal for me. A year later, I was going to have to go to jail for a bit. Since I had gotten arrested in a town called Londonderry, New Hampshire – which was in Rockingham County – I was going to have to do time in the Brentwood County Jail.

At the time, I was fucking a bitch named Stephian that looked like Halle Berry; same haircut, but a phatter...way phatter ass. Raquel, being the down bitch she could be sometimes, made some steak tips and gave me some ass and head. So, I was going into jail with a little bit of a stink on my dick which is always good.

The plea my lawyer got was good for what I was charged with. The most I could do was four months, and Ma Dukes was going to hold down the store while I was gone. Even thought I was as ready as a nigga could be to go to jail, I had never been locked up, so all types of thoughts were going through my head. I didn't worry about being punked cause even though I hadn't worked out in a while, I was 5'10", 250 pounds and my hands were always nice, so a mutherfucker better have packed a lunch because it was going to be a long day if he wanted to test me.

The day that I had court, my mom went with me and I was ready for whatever. I kind of thought that because of my business...my time would get suspended; but the judge didn't see it that way. He was sending my Black ass to jail. The business helped a little though because the judge said I had to serve a mandatory sixty days straight and then six weeks of weekends, which meant I would go to jail on Friday at 6:00 pm and get out on Sunday at 6:00 pm.

Watching the look on my mom's face when I was being taken out of the court, hurt; but I knew she was strong and it wasn't like a nigga just got life. When I arrived to the jail and had to go through the whole booking process and got sent to my sentence block, I kept my cool. It didn't really hit me until my ass was sitting in my cell all by myself with just a Bible and my dick. I once heard an older G say, "As soon as you get there, start to do push-ups," and that's what I did. I banged out probably two hundred for the night. It helped me fall asleep.

When I woke up at 7:00 am to the cell door popping, I thought I was going home, but it was just the punk ass CO bringing me my chow: two hardboiled eggs, some no name cereal and milk. I wasn't hungry, so I put the hardboiled eggs to the side for later and drank the milk. I still couldn't believe that I was in jail. Even though I only had sixty days…trust and believe I lived every day in that box.

My first bid was tough. All I could think about was the streets and all the shit I had done in my life. I had to wait for the Classification Officer to get to me, so I was on twenty-three-hour lockup, with one hour out to shower and work out. By the second day all by myself, I was starting to go a little crazy in my head. The hardest part of it is all the little things that you miss: TV, a fridge, your clothes, cell phone and so on and so on. Since it was a White jail, there were not many Black on the block; actually just two: a Black dude named Rasta and me. He had dreads down to his ass and was a hardcore Rastafarian. He lived the life to the book. He was an old G; fifty years old, but looked about forty. He was serving a year and it wasn't his first bid, so to him, he was on vacation.

On my hour out, he could see the stress on my face. He called me over to his cell and we spoke for a little while and he slipped, *TRUE TO THE GAME II* by Teri Woods under my cell door. He told me to read it and he would get me the other two books. I realized I hadn't read a book in like ten years. I had read a couple of pimp books, but nothing recently. Once I started reading, I fell in love with that book. I couldn't even put it down. The way she writes just flows...not hard, and not easy. Shit...I went through the first hundred pages with ease. I had to put it down so that I had something to do until I got the other two books. I had no idea how long I was going to be on the twenty-three-hour lock up.

That book saved me from going crazy. I could relate to it in every way. The words echoed in my head like a shotgun. There is a part in the book where *Carpe Diem* is mentioned. I had heard the saying, but it wasn't until I was sitting in the box that it hit me. *Seize the day or Seize the moment.* I would later get it tattooed on my wrist where my jail wrist band once rested. There was another part where they quoted Mia Angelou, "I may encounter defeats, but I shall not be defeated." I also got that tattooed on my forearms surrounded by stars; in a star on my right forearm reads, *I may encounter defeats*, and in a star on my left forearm reads, *But I shall not be defeated.* I wasn't going to let this setback break me. I also had to get, *Handle running down* my outer right forearm and *Ur Biz* down my left forearm. I was…and am…going to make that saying famous and my trademark.

At that point, I was addicted to Teri Woods' writing style. All I wanted was the other two books. I had always said I wanted to write a book, but it's easier said than done; which I now know. The first week passed somewhat fast. I would see dudes yelling at their loved ones on the phone and I swore that would never be me, but jail does strange things to you. It takes a while to realize that there's nothing you can do about the shit that is going on in the streets and the people that are living their life on it. They don't call it the stress box for nothing.

Raquel had put $100 on my books and some money on her phone for me to call. Sometimes I look back and wonder where we went wrong. She was a down ass bitch, but I put her through so much, just like R. Kelly said, *A woman scorned.* Stephian also put money on her phone for me to call, but my mother was the first person I spoke to; and just like that, I did what I swore I wouldn't

do My mother hadn't put money on my books yet, and I had left

her with $1,000 for the store. It upset me because a bitch had done

it first, and then I was upset because there were a couple of things

for the store she had not done yet. If you haven't been to jail or

don't know anyone that has been in…putting money on your

phone to receive calls from an inmate can be difficult to handle at

first.

I ended up hanging up the phone mad. To this day, I regret it.

My mother was just as stressed out as me and trying to deal with it

in any way that she could; plus, I left her in charge of the store

which left a lot of responsibility on her hands. She would have to

work seven days a week and take care of all the stress that came

with the store and some of the bills were backed up because of the

$30,000 I gave to the lawyer.

My mother and I have always been close, but this bid would

bring us closer. When you are not running the streets, you have a

lot of time to think and that is just what I did. My mom was always a beautiful woman with a face of a goddess and a body of an angel with a heart of a hustler. Back in the day, her butt had caused a couple of accidents; literally. My mom had a booty and a couple of times when she was younger, men had drove their car into other cars while staring at her. She had me at a young age – nineteen, which until now, I had never thought about how I would have handled a child at that young of an age; especially as a single parent. I know now that I wouldn't have been able to handle it.

My mom held it down for us. She partied, but she always worked at least two jobs trying to support her and me. She got hooked to drugs at a young age after I was born and for about five or six years, she partied hard and I spent a lot of time at my Aunt Fay's house while my mom would disappear for days and sometimes weeks at a time. She would always come back with gifts and money to make up for it. My aunt was also always getting high, so with my three cousins and me in the house, there were times that food was short and there were also times when they would both stay in a room for hours getting high. Shit...I was about six when I realized what drugs were and what they did to families.

At a young age, my cousins: Galen, G, Malik and I swore to never use drugs and to this day, at the age of thirty-five, I can honestly say that I have never tried coke, crack, acid, mushrooms, PCP, Heroin or Mescaline. I have never sniffed a line in my life and I thank my mother for this. Through her addiction and trials and tribulations, I learned she lived and partied for the both of us.

At a very young age, I couldn't understand it at the time, but the time I spent in jail made me realize that my mother made me the man I am today. I wrote her a long letter letting her know that at age thirty-four, I understood that fact and I thanked her for everything she had done to keep us together. I could have easily been in a home or something. Even the way she would gamble after stopping the drugs kept me away from it. I've never been one to gamble and I also thank my mother for that. I owe my mother my life and that is a true story. She was always there for me and now she was holding down the store like a straight G, making sales and placing orders and working six days a week, not leaving until the store had made at least a sale or two. She would take Sundays off, not working the seven days I did, but she was older and she tried the seven days, but found out by the second week that it wasn't that easy. I don't blame her because it's not easy running a Biz and working seven days a week.

My first little bid in jail taught me a lot. Raquel had fallen off after about a month because my mom had got on her nerves and got about $500 out of her for bills. My mom was like a gorilla pimp. After a month, Raquel stayed clear of mom and me; which was all good with me. I had gotten $600 from her and we were not together. She and my mom always bumped heads and to this day, that's probably one of the reasons we are not together. Shit…my mom is my everything. She can get on my nerves, but if you want to be my girl, you gotta smile and put up with it. She is gonna be there for me at the end of the day when all the hoes and the money are gone and she is certified.

Now me and Steph stayed talking through my whole bid, but she had her own issues having a kid and all and being married at like sixteen. I knew it wouldn't last. I've always gone through girls like underwear. She just had to be around when I got out for a little bit of ass. During my sixty days in, I made a lot of goals for myself. I was going to cut back on my drinking and I couldn't smoke because I would be on probation for two years, but that might get cut back to one year because New Hampshire had just passed a law that if you made it halfway through your probation with no violations, you could get off.

I was going to go hard with the store and getting HandleUrBiz.com up and running. I was going to step up the marketing such as Facebook, Twitter and Instagram also as Handle Ur Biz. My whole life was going to be the store; the street life was behind me. I figured that my arrest and the fact that it happened on the day I opened my store was a sign from God for me to stop all the dirt that I was doing. Plus with everything that I had done in the past, and the fact that I was only going to spend about eighty days or so in jail for it, was a sign for me that it was time to stop that life and get out while I could. No smoking, drinking, or sex, can clear a mutherfucker's mind and make him believe he can do all types of things. But life is not that easy. I still had thirty days left of my sixty-day bid. I continued to work out and read through it. I finally got parts I and III of *TRUE TO THE GAME* and I got the *DUTCH* series.

I really loved Teri Woods' writing style and she is banging also. She put her fly ass pic at the end of her books, knowing damn well she looks good. I'm not mad at her. I'm going to do the same thing. She actually got me in a little trouble during my bid. Halfway through, I was moved to a different block and I was given a job in jail laundry. It's a shit job, but it helps break up the bid. A couple of times, I had exchanged a couple of books through the laundry with the dread Rasta, even though it wasn't allowed. On one occasion that I was trying to return the third book in the DUTCH series, the COs went through the laundry cart and found the book and a note. It wasn't serious, but I lost the job and was moved off the block over a fucking book. Jail can be stupid like that sometimes.

At that point, I had fourteen days left, so it didn't really matter to me. I was back on the block with Rasta. He was a real G; he had six months left on his bid and he refused to shave because it was against his religion, so they put his ass on single movement; twenty-three-hour lockdown, one hour out. They were not going to break that dread though; you could pass his cell on a Friday when the college station was playing Reggae and he would be in there rocking back and forth with a smile on his face. He would read the Bible and any other book that he could get his hands on. He ended up doing the rest of his bid in the hole; six months. He wasn't going to break for the White man. I have to give it to that dread, he was a real Rasta.

Well, it was time for my release and you know that Ma Dukes was waiting in the parking lot ready to embrace a mutherfucker. She had been there since 7:00 am, but the jail did not release me until 9:30 am. The first thing I did was hit a store and grab a Gatorade and a Black & Mild and go see my PO to sign

in. then I went straight to my mom's crib to shower the jail off of

me and use my $200 clippers that I missed so much. I threw on my

True Religion jeans and a Sean John tee with some Jordans, my

Armani Exchange Watch, some platinum studs, and a spray of

Armani cologne. Then I was off. The first day out of the joint is

priceless after being locked up for any amount of time. It feels

good to be free. As they say in jail, *You have a glow for that first*

twenty-four hours.

I hit the liquor store next, grabbing a bottle of Hennessy to

sip on while I worked at the store for the day. I also grabbed some

Snapple Iced Tea to mix it with and some more Black & Milds. I

knew it was going to be a long day. I got to the store and pumped

some Max B and a little J-hood to get in the mood while I played a

game or too of Black Ops online. It was good to be home and back

in my store. My mom was going to come down with tons of food

she had made to welcome a brother home. She makes a banging

eggplant lasagna with six cheeses and sauce and meat. It's to die for. She also had a chocolate cake with peanut better frosting, Fried Chicken, and Spanish rice. There is nothing like some home cooking when you get out of jail.

A couple of people came by the store to welcome me home. I ate and sipped all day at the store and chilled with my loved ones. Tomorrow was going to be another day. I was in good spirits. Stephian showed up about 5:00 pm after she got out of work. I closed the store an hour early and had her ride the dick in the back of the store. She was always good for that. Then I was ready for the world; at least that's what I thought. I spent the night at Steph's crib banging it out to the early morning, not getting much sleep. But shit...I had just slept for sixty days. Don't let a nigga from jail fool you...you do a lot of sleeping in jail. Other than lifting weights, reading, playing cards and eating...you are sleeping. So I didn't need it.

I was out the gate like a greyhound my second day. I had merchandise to buy and things to do; plus, in three more days, I would have to turn myself back into jail for those seven weekends that I had ahead of me. I marked off at least five or six different things that I had on my To Do List. I also had my tattoo guy come to the store one night and tat me up. Handle Ur Biz was official. From there on, I was going to live what I preached and Mr. Handle Ur Biz was born.

Chapter 10

Friday came real quick. I was back at the jail ready to turn myself in for the weekend. The whole weekend thing was a blessing and a curse. You are happy that you are not locked up and that you had your freedom, but it was always in the back of your mind that you had to return to jail within four days, so you never really get that full effect of freedom. By the time you got out on Sunday, you could get a couple hours of feeling free, and then you start thinking about Friday all over again.

Each time I got out on Sunday, I would drive straight home to shower and then to the store and sit in the dark and play music and jump online. Once or twice, I turned the open sign on, but Sundays were slow and it was about 8:00 pm by the time I showered and got to the store, so I would just sit and chill and enjoy my freedom and the fact that I was a Biz owner and was accomplishing one of my dreams.

The first two weeks being free went good; everything was falling right into place. I was hitting the gym, I wasn't drinking, I was focused, and I was knocking things off my To Do List that I had made while in jail during my bid. I was really starting to feel good about life and the choices that I was making. I didn't have to look over my shoulder because I wasn't doing any dirt. My mother would watch the store Friday and Saturday when I had to go back to jail. I would head back to jail on Friday at 4:30 to be there by 6:00. I'd grab food and a quick shower and drive myself and park the car at the jail for the weekend.

On my third weekend, I did the same; feeling good with all the things I had accomplished for the week. When I was about one exit away from the jail, I noticed a State Trooper parked in the break down lane. I pulled slightly to the left to give him more than enough space so that if he had to get out of the car, he could. Once I passed him, about ten seconds later, he pulled out behind me. A quick chill went through my body from all the years of riding dirty. I quickly calmed myself down. I wasn't dirty and I was turning myself in for the weekends...doing the right thing. I had nothing to worry about; right?

After a couple of seconds, his lights came on. Again, a chill went through my body. I'm not sure if it is part of getting older or what...but when I was twenty, I would ride dirty with drugs, a burner, and no license, all while smoking a blunt and I never thought twice. I pulled over on the right shoulder thinking that he would pass, but he didn't. I grabbed my license and registration and waited for him to approach.

When he came up, I asked, "Officer, why am I being pulled over?"

He said, "A new law has been passed. When an officer is in the break down lane, you need to pull over to the far left lane."

For a second, I started to tell him that I moved over as much as possible, but there was a car next to me, but I decided to save my breath. I thought I would just get a warning, knowing that the real reason that he pulled me over was because I was Black and he wanted to check if I had warrants. I knew the plates were good. The car was in my mother's name...like I always did.

He asked, "Is your license good?"

"Yes," I said, knowing that my mother had paid a fine for me when I did my sixty days.

The cop came back about five minutes later and said, "I thought you told me your license was good?"

"It is."

"It's suspended. Step out of the car."

I was in shock. *What the fuck?!* I thought I was doing everything right. Why was God punishing me? I stepped out of the car. My mind was going crazy.

"Step to the back of the car and place your hands behind your back," the officer said.

I did, and within seconds, I was in handcuffs and placed in the back of the police cruiser. I couldn't believe it. When I did my sixty days, I prayed to God telling Him I would not break any laws and asking Him to keep an eye on me, and there I was in handcuffs again.

Fuck me!

I knew getting arrested was a violation of my probation. I was shitting bricks. I had a three-to-five bid hanging over my head. I explained to the cop that I was on my way to the jail to turn myself in for the weekend. I saw a spark in his eyes. He thought I was a punk ass convict and was going to try to get me to snap. He made a call on his cell. I knew it wasn't to the dispatcher because he would have used the radio. I figure the call was to his wife or girlfriend, telling them that his shift was about to end and that he was going to be late because he just pulled someone over and their license was suspended and they were on their way to jail to turn themselves in for the weekend and that he had to take me there. I could hear the lady laugh literally out loud.

My blood was boiling. When he hung up the phone, I said with a little attitude that I was glad that the lady thought my life was so funny. You would think that he would have realized that what just happened was unprofessional and take it easy on me, but no...he probably figured that I would snap any second and he would have me right where he wanted me. But I had dealt with dickhead COs and cops like him before. I would kill him with kindness.

He started to ask all types of questions that he could have got from the jail. *Where do you work? Do you still live at the same address? What is your full name? Do you have any tats? What were you in jail for*....and so on and so on. I wanted to yell, *Mutherfucker, just take my ass to jail*, but I knew that is what he wanted so I kept quiet.

When we arrived at the jail, my bail was $40; which I had on me, but I still had to stay for the weekend. It was the longest weekend ever. All I could think about was violating my probation. I got out on Sunday and my mother had called the registry of Motor Vehicles to find out what happened when she paid the fine. They told her that even though she had paid the fine, there was a reinstate fee of $150. It cost me $40 for the bail, $150 for the reinstatement, $250 for the tow, and $750 for the fine of driving after suspension. A grand total of $1,200 is what I was hit with. I went on Monday and paid it all. It was a major setback seeing as though I had only been out of jail for two weeks, and then I still had to go see my Probation Officer.

I was sweating bullets once I got into the PO's office. My PO was cool though, he told me that since I went right away and squared things away, he assumed that I really didn't know that I didn't have my license and it was just bad luck on my part. He said that he wasn't going to have my probation violated. I breathed a sigh of relief and thanked him and God and went on my way.

The last couple of weekends went without any problems. I had been released from jail eight times since serving my sixty days. I was glad to get that shit over with. It was time to Handle Biz. I made a couple of trips to New York to grab merchandise from the store even though I shouldn't have left the state without my PO's permission, but I figured my bad luck was over. Shit...I was doing everything else right; no smoking weed, so my piss was clean, no drinking and I even stopped smoking Black & Milds. I was on point and hit the gym often. What could go wrong? Ever since my arrest for driving after suspension and losing $1,200, I had put away $3,000 and the store was packed. I was making a lot off of knockoff Northface. I was getting them in New York for $15 and selling them for $80. They were going like crack. The stores sold them for $180, so I was getting all types of new customers; White, Spanish, Black, Asian...everyone seemed to like Northface. I don't know what the big deal was. In my day, the Triple Fat Goose Jackets were hot; at least they had down feathers.

Anyway, I was moving like forty of them a week and pulling in $3,200 just from them alone. A couple more weeks and I would be sitting on $10,000 easy. I was going to make a power move and sell the car I had, so on this trip I could buy more and double my profit and it would save me my weekly trip to New York. I would be without a car for a week, but with the money I would make, I could grab something hot; maybe a Beemer or Jag again. I had done the same thing many times while selling drugs. Shit...I was a hustler; it was the way I had always lived...except this time it was just another hustle.

I sold my whip and had just enough money to buy 200 jackets. I just paid all my bills, so I was all caught up and I would pull in about $16,000 or $14,500 if I sold some for lesser amounts. Ever since catching my charge, paying lawyer fees and owning the store, I hadn't had more than $1,500 in the stash. I was about to be back on my feet and it had only taken me two months after my release from jail to do it. It was also a couple weeks before Thanksgiving; the biggest shopping season of the year and at the rate that the jackets were going, I could make three or four more trips before Christmas. The money I could have stacked before the end of the year was crazy. This was it...I was going to be back on top.

When I got back from New York, I was ready. I grabbed a couple other things also like G-Shock watches, Jordans, Air Forces, hoodies and a couple other things; but most, if not all of my money was put into the jackets. The first couple of days, I sold about twenty jackets. At that rate, I would be able to make another trip in a week if I didn't buy a whip, and *fuck a whip*…the more money I made, the phatter car I could buy.

One day while at the store hanging out with this chic, Amanda – who would be one of the first of the three girls that would get the Handle Ur Biz tat – a White male came in the store. I immediately got a strange feeling about him as he walked to the rack with the jackets on them. Not only was I so hung over from the night before, but a lot of people did that…just walking over to the jackets. Word was out on the street that I had them and most people knew what they wanted and normally, my clientele for the store was urban kids from twelve to thirty. With these jackets, it wasn't abnormal for a forty to sixty year old white man or woman to come in to buy one for their son, daughter or grandkid; so when he picked up a pink one, I quickly through the funny feeling out and went into sale pitch mode.

He had two of them in his hands by the time I walked up; a pink one and a white one. I had them in all colors; black, purple, brown, baby blue…every color. He had a size XS in his hands, so I assumed it was for a twelve-year-old girl. He told me his daughter wanted one. I explained that the white ones got dirty quick and that if she was a kid, maybe he should grab the pink one and if she took good care of it, that he should come back for the white one and I would cut him a deal. He was sold. He handed over the $80, I bagged it up and he was gone. I turned back to continue talking to Amanda about whatever we were talking about before the sale, probably me...I did that a lot. Plus, I was feeling good; it was the seventh jacket that I had sold that day and it wasn't even 1:00 pm yet. At the rate I was going, I would rake in another $800 or more by the end of the day and with a 75% profit margin, I was tripling my money. I was on a money high. All hustlers know about that.

My homegirl, Nicole, walked in a couple of minutes later. She had to go to Toys R Us and my PS3 had just shit the bed, so I peeled off $200 for a new one and sent her on her way. About a half an hour later, the White man came back and right behind him was a Nashua Police Officer. My heart started to pound. I didn't know what was up.

"Do you remember me?" the White man asked.

"Yes, especially now that you have a cop walking behind you."

"Can I talk to you alone?"

I quickly turned to Amanda and told her to wait in the back of the store. As soon as she left, the man explained to me that he was a Private Detective for big companies such as Northface and others. He was not there to arrest me, but had brought the cop with him just as a witness. He then went on to say that I needed to take the knockoff jackets off the rack and I didn't have to give them up, but it would show good faith to Northface if I did and he would promise that a lawsuit wouldn't follow.

My mind was going every which way. I went from such a high to such a low in a very short period of time. I was still on probation, so I didn't want any problems. Shit...if I got in trouble again, I was sure to get violated. While I was talking to the two men, a girl came in and went to the rack with the jackets. I told the detective to hold on. I walked over to the girl and tried to explain what was happening.

She said, "I don't care about that. I'll take two of them."

"I can't sell them to you," I said and she walked out the store with her $160. It was definitely a sad day and it was something that I would have to get used to because over the next couple of weeks, I had to turn down more than 100 people for those jackets. Well, I stopped counting at 100. A lot of people would have bought two or more, so at that rate, I would have been sold out six days later. Shit...why couldn't they have come before the Detective and Cop? I mean...well, I gave up the jackets, which I later regretted. The Detective and the Cop asked a few questions when I turned over the jackets and I just told them that I bought them off of some African in New York and that I didn't know his name. I really did know his name, but those pigs didn't need to know that.

I signed a couple of papers and was told someone would be back to check to make sure that I wasn't selling the jackets any more or I would get arrested. That made me look at all of the 100 people that came in the store strange and give them a slight attitude when they came looking for the jackets over the next month. I wasn't even able to stop the attitude. It was like a smack in the face seeing money walk out and not knowing if they were undercovers or not. It kind of made me sick to my stomach.

People would walk in and ask about the jackets. When I said that I didn't have them anymore, they would just leave; not even looking at the other merchandise. When the Detective left, he gave me some good advice that I followed. He told me he noticed a couple of knockoff from other companies and I should get rid of them. He said he really didn't care, but he wanted to just give me a head's up.

Thanks Buddy, is all I thought as I watched him walk out the door with $14,000 of my money. *Charge it to the game*, I thought as he left. Being a hustler for so long, you get used to that saying. It helps ease the pain when you get beat. I had only been out of jail two months and got my paper up and lost it just that quick. $14,000 plus 1,200 = $15,000; and my Christmas plans were a hit and now I had no car. I got rid of all the other knockoff items: Louie Vuitton, Prada, Gucci...everything and I barely made my money back. It was going to be a bad end to the year for sure.

I knew I couldn't give up though. I had it tattooed on my forearms...*I may encounter defeats, but I shall not be defeated.* I had definitely just encountered a defeat by the hand of the man...I would have rather gotten robbed by a stick-up kid. At least that way I could have got a punch in.

Over the next couple of months, my faith in doing the right thing was tested. I was approached by at least four chicks looking for a little guidance, which you know what that means to a pimp. It was on the fourth one that made me say, *Fuck it!* I can't even remember her name. A friend of mine called me about her saying that she needed to make money for a ticket to move back to Florida and if I knew a couple of people....she would give me a cut. I told him to bring her by the store.

All a pimp needs is a bottom bitch (Main Chick) to make thousands. Let's see what she is about. I've learned for every ten bitches you get…maybe one or two will really work out and even less of them are bottom bitches, so I didn't have high hopes; especially seeing that I didn't pull her on my own. Don't get me wrong, I've gotten a couple that brought to me that made a G or two.

When my boy came in the store, the girl came in behind him. She was maybe a five; blond hair, an ok face and some big ass tits. She did have some dick sucking lips for a White girl though. I would find out later that's what she mainly did with her tricks. I turned the light off at the store and sat and talked to her for a while. I had a blue light that shined on the sneakers and wall that said, *Handle Ur Biz* in graffiti. She was down to make money and would give me half of what she made if I set it up and 25% of what she set up. She planned on leaving for Florida in two weeks, so it wasn't going to be a long-term thing. I didn't mind. I just wanted some money to pay some bills at the store.

We both spent the night at the store and drank and talked. She was only twenty-five, but she had been through a lot. She knew the game. She had been a hoe since she was sixteen. The next day I got on the phone trying to set shit up. Right next door to my store was a Chinese Restaurant and the Asian dude that worked the desk was always looking for a bitch and he would pay. He was used to crackhead bitches, so it was a battle to get $80 for some head out of him, but I got it. I told him it was worth every second, even though I did not know if it was or not. He stopped by the store after the lunch rush around 2:30 pm and he was out of my bathroom by 2:33 pm. I was like, Damn...she must be good. I told her I only got $40 so I gave her $20 and kept $60. It's part of the game. Don't hate the playa, hate the game, I thought to myself. I knew the Chinese dude would be back within a couple of days.

Next, my younger cousin stopped by the store. He is a good-looking kid at twenty-one. It runs in the family. I had gotten him head from at least seven or eight hoes that I had working for me in the past. He loved his big cousin. I wanted to see if that bitch got him off that quick since he was good looking. The hoe didn't hesitate to go in the bathroom when I told her to, even though she wasn't getting paid.

Fucking hoes...gotta love them.

I was surprised. My cousin seemed to come out even quicker than the Chinese dude did. After seeing that, I wanted to find out for myself, but I was gonna wait till we made more money. I've always loved money over hoes. *You can get hoes chasing money, but you can't get money chasing hoes*, like Nas said.

My mind frame paid off over the next week and a half. I made $1,500 fucking with that bitch. She bought her ticket to Florida and the night before she left, we partied at the store with a bottle of Grey Goose. Her head game was serious. She knew what she was doing. She looked you straight in the eyes the whole time; plus, she would hum on it. She used both hands; one moving up and down the cock in a circular motion, and the other playing with your balls. She was a pro for sure. I dropped her off the next morning at the airport in a car that I was using from one of my boys. I haven't seen or heard from her since. Sometimes it's like that with hoes.

The money was gone quicker than it came. $1,000 on rent for the store and $200 on cable for the store and $300 on the gas; that's how it usually went with owning a Biz, as soon as it comes in…it goes out to bills, rent, and living expenses. I've heard many people say that they would never want to own a Biz because at least with a regular job, they are guaranteed a check at the end of the week. I think that in a lot of ways, they are right; but the feeling of owning your own Biz is great; especially when you are talking about it to others that you just met. There is no way to say that you are a business owner without confidence; even if the business is doing badly and you are living in the store like I was. It really didn't bother me though, I didn't have any kids and I knew it was part of owning a business. Not having a shower sucked and not having a full bed sucked too, but other than that…*Fuck it, I've been in jail*, so this was much better than that.

Chapter 11

Over the next couple of months, I was keeping it legit. I had to see my PO each month and I was almost half way through, so I wanted to stay out of trouble so that I could try to get off probation early. I wanted to try a little hood marketing, so I got this hoe chick that I was fucking named, Amanda, to tattoo *Handle Ur Biz* on her rib cage surrounded by a rose. She had about 3,000 friends on Facebook and I had about the same, so I knew people would be talking about it. I was right, within a week, I got my homeboy's sister to tattoo it right above her pussy and when I posted a picture, more people started to talk. A buzz was going around about the store; good or bad, it was a way of promotion and marketing.

The third girl came about two weeks after the others. She was known as Puerto Rican Rumm on Facebook. That bitch was crazy, but she had about 5,000 friends on Facebook. When she got it on her ass, dudes were coming in left and right asking me how I got her to do it. I simply told them that if I told them how, then they would be doing it and I couldn't have that. People were commenting on the pics; good and bad. All three girls stuck up for themselves. People didn't believe me, but I had only fucked Amanda. The others I just talked into doing it for me. The whole thing actually turned into a nice little soap opera for the people on my page because Amanda and Puerto Rican Rumm didn't like each other, so they would fight constantly on my page. At the time, the Drake song was out, "Tat My Name on you to show that it's real."

I was a hood legend in many eyes; both fans and haters...either way, they were talking. Biz got a little better, but it wasn't enough. I needed to do something else to keep the store going and it had to be legal. I didn't want to get caught up. Sometimes you make decisions in the moment because it seems like the best or only thing to do, and this was one of those moments.

I knew a dude that had his own music label called Fam Music. He was a Puerto Rican cat. They called him Face. I went to school with his brother, RedRum. Rum was cool. I never really dealt with Face before; especially on some money making shit. People can be as cool as the other side of the pillow, but when it comes to money, everyone Handles Biz differently.

The deal was that Face would give me $1,000 and build a studio in the store. I'd get 30% of what was brought in by the studio. The split was supposed to be 30% for Face, 30% for me, 30% for the sound man, and 10% for promotion. Face would supply everything for the studio; mic, computer, programs, inbox, sound pro, material, and etc.; and he would eventually pay me another $9,000 over a period of time to be 40% owner of the store. I would always have the most stock, 60% so that I always had the last word.

Everything started good. He had a team of felons. They would follow his every move. He always rolled three to four deep and he had a big following seeing that he was in his own rap group of four dudes. There was Ant Live, Spaz, RedRum, and Face. They were all cool and they also did their solo things. I was always into music, so it looked like a sound idea.

When it all started there were late night sessions at the store, drinking, building the studio, freestyle rapping and just bugging out. It was all fun and games at first. What I didn't know at the start was Fam was known as a street gang more than a music label. Well, I kind of knew, but I didn't know that the police had it out for those dudes. Face had done five years Upstate for drugs and the rest of the crew had rap sheets as long as they were.

The police started to patrol the street a little more and on a couple of the late night sessions, they knocked on the door to check if things were alright. At least, that is what they claimed. Teaming up with Face was bringing more police than customers; plus the dude had beef with a lot of people. His family was big and seeing that he was from New York and had the New York attitude to go with it.

The studio was taking longer to get up than I thought. Only the people on his label were using it and they didn't pay, so I wasn't seeing any money from it. The late night sessions were getting old; it's hard to kick a broke, drunk, felon out. They just don't want to leave. My nights and days were getting longer and my pockets were getting smaller. His entourage turned into squatters once Face went home. It was only about a month and a half into it and it was starting to get real old.

Around that time, a White boy that I had been locked up with called and when we were locked up, he had talked about getting a check for $15,000 and that he wanted to use some of it to invest in the store. A lot of people said that shit in jail, so I never took it too seriously until he showed up with his girl . She was a Cap Verde chick: she was pretty with long dark hair the same texture as a mixed Black and White girl. She had the color and complexion of a Spanish girl and a tight little runner's body to go along with it. I am not sure what she saw in him, but…whatever.

He was a rapper, so the thing I had going with the studio and the Fam Music label seemed like a perfect fit. I'm not going to lie…the White boy had some fire from being locked up so much. He had notebooks and notebooks of shit(RIP JOSH L). He knew he would only have a small share for his investment of $4,500. He was going to work hours with me at the store. So now I had two partners. I thought that would take some of the stress off of me, but I was wrong. The White boy was never on time. He was getting high on pills and heroin and he was pussy whipped. He was going to be broke in a couple of weeks. I could see it coming.

Face was just trying to do too much. He had a good mouth game like me, so he could get things done or at least make you believe they were getting done, but he was just doing too many other things at the same time. His mother had also just passed away, and a local snitch dude was fucking with him hard, trying to get him to snap so that he could catch another charge.

I needed to make something happen and it had to be big. Face had a hookup on another location on Main Street and the owner of it had apartments upstairs from the place. So I could finally move out the store. We had just gotten the White boy an apartment there and there was an open storefront and the landlord said he wouldn't put us in one store and custom build the other one for use. The landlord was a really shady business man, which I wouldn't find out till much later.

I swear you don't make it anywhere in business unless you do some dirt, like my father once said.

I was still on probation, so I needed to watch what I did. All the felons I was hanging out with were violations in themselves; plus…me planning on getting the apartment and the other thing…I knew I had to decide something soon. I could either pay my back rent and bills, or take the chance on a different spot. I had already decided to change the name of the store and use the *Handle Ur Biz* name for my own projects. Shit…I was *Mr. Handle Ur Biz,* I wanted to start a clothing line, get my website running better and it was something that I didn't have to share with those two fools. Not to mention, I had built the name. There was no reason for them to profit off of my hard work.

It was moments and actions like this that made me say that things happen for a reason.

One day while I was sitting at the store, the landlord called. She was an older Brazilian lady. I had kissed her ass for the last two years of owning the Biz; that arrest had really fucked me up. I was always paying my rent late, but it was always paid. I was $2,000 late this time around, but I was sitting on $4,500 when she called and tried to get hard with me giving me a week to come up with the money or she was taking over my store. She said I better have all of her money by the next Tuesday, and it was Tuesday when she called.

I sat there and listened to that bitch, and all I could think was, *She don't know me. I have done all types of things in a week.* Not only had she just given me too much time, but she was threatening me, and I hate to be threatened. She didn't know it, but she had just made up my mind for me about getting the apartment above the new store location that I was planning on moving us all to. I told her that I would have the money on Monday. By the time I hung up, my mind was in motion. I called Face and told him to tell the Landlord guy that we would be taking the spot on Main Street and

I also explained to him that we would be moving out like thieves in the middle of the night on Sunday.

Over the years, I have moved out on landlords and girlfriends in the middle of the night; now I was adding a store to the list. It didn't bother me in the least. *Fuck that bitch Landlord...now she gets nothing from me.* The store on Main Street was two times bigger and with the apartment upstairs, the rent was going to be twice as much, but *Fuck it!* It is Main Street – one of the top three busy spot for a business in Nashua with lots of foot traffic and the spot to be to run a biz – and I would think about that shit when it came down to it. If I was going to have to make some moves in order to make things happen, then that's what I would have to do.

Sunday came and I was leaving the store that I had been in for two years. It was kind of a sad moment, but I was hoping for the best. In a way, I was hoping my bad luck would be over. Ever since I had signed the lease on that place, it had been downhill from there. Getting arrested on the day I opened was either real bad luck, or a sign from God, or both. I'm not sure, but it had my

mind very uneasy about life and the choices I had made.

Chapter 12

I hate to stop the book like this again, but I'm trying to keep you updated on my current situation and show you how hard jail life is and the obstacles it brings with it. It took me months to bunk up with my boy Paulie V.; which I'll talk about him more later in the book. A bitch ass CO named Lucy…that is a bipolar Puerto Rican bitch…split us up after a couple of weeks just to be a punk ass CO. Sometimes the COs do shit like that to try and break a nigga. I didn't argue. I kept my cool. Paulie V. got a twenty-three hour lockup for bugging out on the CO. Shit…she deserved it. They moved me into an older White man's cell. He had rubbed me the wrong way weeks before, so I had nothing to say to the guy when I got into the cell.

In any other jail, I could have smacked him up; but in this country ass jail, inmates press charges against other inmates. I stayed away from my new celly all day, trying to just tell myself that I was short time. That's what inmates consider 100 days or less on a sentence. One bad move and I would lose my good time of four months…120 days. I did not want that to happen because then I would be back to where I started.

When he came in the room at lock in, I put down what I was writing and went to sleep. I could hear him up writing and flipping through books. He must have fallen asleep at midnight, because at about 12:05 am, I woke up to the loudest snoring and gasping for air that I had ever heard. I thought someone was dying. He also talked in his sleep. Between the snoring and gasping for air, he would say, "Yup, yup, yup." It was killing me and to top it off, he had restless leg syndrome where he would rub his legs like a cricket.

I was in jail inside of a jail. I yelled for the CO. It happened to be one I was cool with. When he came to the cell door, he could hear the sound from the cell and he moved me at 12:30 am to an empty cell on the bottom tier. I just took my mat and blankets. No flip flops, just socks. I told the CO that I would get my shit in the morning. 6:00 am came quick. I showered, shaved for work and still didn't grab my stuff. I had to wait till the first shift arrived.

Finally, I was moved after breakfast to my cell with Paulie V. A couple of days passed with the old White man making bullshit conversation which I gave him small talk just because I was happy I was out of his cell.

Finally it was time to go into my canteen bag to grab more coffee. I had noticed the bag wasn't how I had tied it, but I chalked it up to the move. Well, to make a long story short, a cell thief is the worst. I was missing a bag of Columbian coffee. A $6 bag at that. Everything counts in jail. I knew for sure that the thief was not my man Paulie V. It had to be the older White guy because he was a teacher that got hooked on coke and robbed all his neighbors for jewelry and got caught and charged with receiving stolen property. The problem was…if I smashed the man, I would get more charges and wouldn't get to go home like I planned. At this point in time, I have eighty-nine days and a wake up left.

What do I do? Should I risk my time off for good behavior over a bag of coffee or just keep it moving?

Well, I'll let you know how that ends by the end of the book.

Chapter 13

So where was I?

I've moved the store to Main Street. The new name was going to be Finesse. We started to build the studio and planned on opening two weeks later after all the right paperwork was filled. I started to notice that the dude, Face, was doing less and less, but had his people believing he was doing more and more. The $1,000 was all I had received from him, but I was patient seeing that he had gotten the spot for a low price.

The White boy that gave the $4,500 was almost ghost around the store. We saw him less and less. A lot of the dudes that were hanging around were hitting on his girl and he had no heart. He was also broke. He had spent the $15,000 in five weeks, just like I knew he would. *Damn fool!*

I chilled for the two weeks and hired a couple of girls to work the store, but I quickly realized that old saying, *If you want something done right, you have to do it yourself.* So I was back to working more hours. The studio was taking forever. No money was coming in from the studio or from Face. I was quickly realizing that it was a bad move hooking up with him in the first place. He wasn't working any hours and was bringing a bad heat to the store. His entourage was a bunch of drunks that needed to be kicked out of the store at least once a week for showing up too drunk to get anything done.

Things were quickly getting out of hand. The store wasn't making any money. All I could think was, *What have I done?*

I applied to get off of probation early. My PO had no problem putting in the paperwork. I hadn't pissed dirty and no violations. I thought I would be off of probation in no time, but in the meanwhile, I needed to make some moves. A White girl named Mellisa, but they called her Loca, came to me like many girls had before, saying, "You're not my pimp or anything, but I need someone with me and I'll throw you a cut."

Shit...whateva makes you sleep at night.

Over the next few weeks, I let Face and another girl run the store while Loca and I placed ads online and drove up and down from Mass to New Hampshire pulling tricks and staying in hotels. The store wasn't making much money; which wasn't a surprise to me. *Why did I ever team up with that dude?* Was my thought process on a daily bases. The only biz that the studio had since I had started up the partnership was his people it was getting old quick. I ended my two weeks with Loca bringing in only $1,200, but it was free money. I put it toward the store trying to keep it alive.

I found out that I had gotten denied for early probation because I had gotten arrested when I was driving to do the weekend stays in jail. I was crushed. Things were still not going my way, so I vented like I always do by fucking every bitch I could, then getting sick of them and throwing them away.

The White boy had totally disappeared from the store and would call asking for money. I hit him off a couple of times with $200, but I had mad bills and I knew he was getting high, so I told him he was going to have to wait.

Face and I started to bump heads more and more. He swore he was doing something with the store, but I just didn't see it, while I was working over eighty hours a week; seven days a week. I still hadn't received any money and the studio wasn't looking any better, but I had a couple more tricks up my sleeve before I was gonna bow out.

The store was so big; I could rent out spaces to other people. I first got a guy that had a T-Mobile franchise on board. I charged him $300 and he was to have the back of the store. The problem with him was that he was spreading himself thin. Also, he had two rents to pay at two different locations and he was working a regular job, so he was paying two different people to run them. He was going nowhere fast; plus, he wasn't doing any marketing or promotion. He lasted two months. The $600 helped out, but it wasn't enough.

Next came a White boy that made T-shirts. Face actually found him, so you already know how that played out. The dude paid $400 for two months and was making the sign for the store.

Needless to say, the sign was complete before his T-shirts, so he didn't work out either, but the $400 helped; just not enough.

The third one to come through was a Spanish guy and his girl. They paid $300 for the month and sold women's accessories, pocket books, wallets, dress shoes – both men's and women's. They started off strong; working every day, but then they wanted me to sell their shit and give them the money. That wasn't the deal, even though they were paying rent.

Now I'm working for you? I don't think so!

I knew that wasn't going to work out. They lasted two months, so that was another $600. But that wasn't enough. My bills at the store were about $2,000, so all the money was just enough to keep me pretty much running around in circles only to end up right where I started. To top it all off, Face showed up at the store to talk and he wanted out.

Shit...I bet you do!

He wasn't working doing shit anyway, but I think he had lost his fucking mind. He was going to take all his studio shit; which I knew that, but that fool wanted his $1,000 back. We had been in Biz for about eight months and I had spent the $4,500 that the White boy gave me and the $1,200 I made with Loca, plus my eighty hours a week and anything else I had done on the side. I was easily $15,000 into the store and 3,000 hours spent on it and that fool wanted $1,000. He didn't want it right at that moment. He thought he was doing me a favor by saying he would take it in $100 payments here and there as I had it.

It took everything in me not to smack the shit out of him, but he would be gone, so I just yupped him to death between him and his drunk entourage and his beef on the streets.

Good riddens! The mutherfucker was crazy.

I was not sure what I was going to do. I had a lot on my mind.

*****

I hate to stop the book again, but the old white man just knocked on my cell door to say that he had heard I was missing coffee and that he didn't have it. News on a jail block spreads like high school news and I knew he would deny it. He is a convict. They do that. When you are in jail, an inmate or convict knows what he has. It is not like you own a lot in jail. All of your property can fit in one or two trash bags. You know what books you have, how much soap, deodorant, lotion, oatmeal, soups and especially coffee you have. Those small things are your world. That shit is like crack in jail and you know your own personal inventory.

His words bubbled over inside me. I didn't expect him to say anything different than what he said, but it still angered me.

I'm still not sure how I am going to handle it. I'll let you know. Don't worry...rule one when you are in jail...you have to Handle Ur Biz.

*****

Now back to the situation at the Main Street store...Face was gone, but we were still cool. Biz was slow and the bills were stacking up. I was still on probation, so my options were slim. At that point, it was hard for me to stress. All I could do was go with the flow; good or bad. Something had always happened for me to turn things around, so I knew it was just a matter of time. Besides, I was a pimp. I couldn't lose my cool; right?

I spent the next couple of weekends getting drunk and fucking bitches. What else can a hood nigga do? I had taken what money I had left and hit the landlord off. I was caught up in the store, but late on the apartment. I also put money on the electricity. I had two weeks to come up with more money for that, or I would get cut off from that too.

I was getting a little worried, but like Ma Dukes always said, *Keep the Faith.* At times like this, I would start to think about how things would have played out if the White boy had never worn a wire on me on my opening day. *Where would I be?* I could have gotten into bigger trouble, or I could have made enough money to get out of the game. Only God knows. *Whatever doesn't kill you makes you stronger;* right?

I had a lot of questions and not enough answers. Things were about to happen and I didn't know it was the beginning of the end.

I ended up showing up to work just like any other day, trying to keep the faith, and a little after 1:00 pm, the Mexican dude, Jaime, that owned the store, Urban Zone, had showed up with his little son. They were hanging out on one of the couches in the store and he explained that he had someone running his store and he planned on moving to Texas in a couple of months. He said he was just bored with where he was. He also said that the guy that he had running his store was doing really good and he was just sitting at home and wanted to keep busy.

He asked if I was willing to let him set up shop at my store for the next month, maybe longer. *Now was this what I was waiting for? I needed money, and him bringing in new merchandise could only help; right?*

He asked more questions that I didn't know the answers to, but fuck it…"Let's do this," I said.

I would live to regret that decision later on; and a lot sooner than I thought. Jaime set up shop in the back of the store and I knew from the start that I had underestimated the man that I had looked at as a friend. He was never my friend. That was something that I would find out real soon.

Jaime brought in so much merchandise that it made my stuff look like Flea Market shit. I knew I was fucked from the start. The first day, which was the first of the month, went well for both of us. With the SSI checks and welfare checks in the pockets of customers, we both did well. I made about $600 for the day and he did about the same. Maybe I had a chance. *Maybe this could work out,* I thought to myself.

The next couple of days showed that I was seriously wrong. I had $20 days and he had $200. Then I would have a $40 day and he would have a $300 day. At that rate, I would never be able to pay my half of the rent. I had to raise his rent up $200. Being a business man, he didn't want to give it up, but he knew he was going to make it right back. It was the third of the month and he had doubled that amount already. It was a win/win situation for him and he still had twenty-eight days left within the month.

The next couple of days were the worst for me. $10, $5, and then nothing. Jaime was making all the money. I couldn't compete with him in my own store. But since I thought that he was my friend, I had hoped that maybe he would help me out and cuff me the merchandise he had and I could pay him monthly. There were a lot of things that we could have worked out if he was a friend; but there are no friends when it comes to Biz. There is just Biz.

Within a week, he knew that he was on the verge of putting me out of business. He sat there like a shark in the water waiting. Cash is king when you are sitting on enough money that you can just sit back and be comfortable, and that is just what he did. He came to work every day and stole my sales. I can't even say it was stealing since I invited him in. I knew I had made a big mistake. I treated him like the other small biz guys and he definitely was not one.

He sat back all those years listening to me brag about bitches and money and was about to destroy me. He knew what he was doing. I could see then how Mom and Pop stores get taken out by bigger, stronger and richer companies. I was fucked.

A week and a half into it, and I had nothing saved up. I had had a couple of days where I didn't sell a thing. I was slowly dying. There wasn't much for me to do. I had tried to stay in business for almost three years. After catching a charge on my opening day, I went to jail, I got arrested, and I got hit for $1,200, then lost everything damn near with that Northface thing. In my head, I rationalized that I had done all I could. I had had a good run...now it was time for me to make an offer to Jaime. I figured if I made him an offer to buy me out, I could bow out gracefully. That way, I wouldn't have failed if I didn't really go out of business.

I sold out.

I knew it wasn't going to be easy to get a lump sum out of that bastard, so I was going to hit him with a low number. With that, I could go to New York, grab shit and sell it out the trunk of my ride. I was a hustler...I wouldn't be just sitting in one place. I'd be mobile with no overhead other than gas. I could make it happen.

I could work on my clothing line, get my website going and I could

always make the worst thing sound good. I was a pimp.

Business is cut throat. The amount I asked for to give up the

shop was reasonable. I only asked for $3,000 and that was for all

my racks, merchandise, surveillance, kicks, open signs and all

other type of shit. The number he came back with was a smack in

the fucking face...$1,500. It took everything in me for me not to

smack him, but he knew if I didn't take that, I would take nothing

when the whole place was closed down. Probation is a bitch. I had

three to five years over my head, so I couldn't even get gangster

with that dude because I couldn't take the chance. I was fucked.

He definitely was not my friend; he proved that. He had so

much money that $3,000 wouldn't hurt him. I even tried to get

$500 more by negotiating with him, but he wouldn't go for it. I

told him I would help with promotion on my Facebook, Twitter

and Instagram pages and he still wouldn't go for it.

I have to give it to the dude, Face...when I told him how everything went on, he had my back. He said for me to give him the word and it would be on. And it could have been. I could have easily taken all Jaime's merchandise he had in the store and put the goons on him. I didn't do it because I did not know if he would call the cops. I had time over my head and I couldn't take the chance.

$1,500...I've been broker than that before. I can make that work, I told myself. Not to mention...*what other options do I really have?*

I was going to take it. I still would have the apartment. I'd hit the landlord with the $300 I owed him and have $1,200 to flip. I was going to get back in the game. Well, I made a couple of last minute mistakes. The landlord thought I was getting more, so he added almost $500 to the apartment and since I paid him weekly for that, I never kept the receipts; my bad. And I was going to get back in the game somehow. I forgot that I hadn't pumped in two years. I had the connect; I just didn't have the clientele.

I made the deal with the dickhead, Jaime, aka Urban Zone, and then I paid the landlord and told him he would have the rest in a week. That bought me some time. I had bumped into one of my runners, so I told him he could move in my crib and push some shit. What I didn't know was that he started shooting the shit. So after stealing his customers and making $1,000 in a week, I kicked his ass out. He was too much trouble; it wasn't worth it. I would have killed that kid and caught another charge. I ducked the landlord for another week and made another $1,000; he wasn't getting any more money from me. I bought an Audi A6 2004 that would work for a while and I moved to Ma Dukes' crib for a week or two until I got enough money together for an apartment.

My PO just switched me to minimum status, so I had to go every three months and I only had ten months left. I would be done in no time. Things were looking up; at least, that's what I told myself. I called some of the old people that I used to fuck with, but a lot of them were clean; the others just were not spending that much money. I needed to register the Audi; plus, I had taken a trip to New York and bout a new wardrobe. I had to look good if I was back in the game. I started to hit the club and bars more; strip clubs too…but I wanted and needed to get my money up before I was really ready for a stripper in my life.

Money was coming in so slow. It had been a month since I sold the store and I was hearing that Jaime was running his mouth to some of my loyal customers. That wasn't resting well with me. Then he tried to tag me on Facebook with some new merchandise that he had gotten, which he had actually stolen my ideas. He was the same dude that couldn't give me $500 more, but could tag *Handle Ur Biz* in his pics. That wasn't going to work. I sent him a message in his inbox and told him to untag me and delete me.

I wanted to kill him. I went on Facebook and told people, "Jaime from Urban Zone can suck my dick."

People must have told him because he texted me asking what had he done. I couldn't even text him back. I was on fire.

What had he done? This mutherfucker needed an ass whoppin'. The more and more I thought about it, the more I got pissed off. I wanted to kill him. He had definitely taken advantage of the situation; but Biz is Biz, I guess.

I was thirty-four years old and living at home. I was on probation, with a 2004 Audi A6 which I owned and about $400 to my name. I had a new wardrobe and not much Biz. *What the fuck happened?* The Audi alone was going to be $300 just to register it. It would be another month or so before I could get an apartment seeing that the coke I had gotten was moving slow. I didn't want to be hanging at my mom's house dirty, so I was out more; which meant I was spending more and even though it's rare in my life, but I wasn't fucking with too many chicks, so even my chick game was at an all-time low.

I felt like the walls were closing in on me. When I sit in jail now and think about it…it wasn't that bad; but at the time, it was. I had been through a lot over the last couple of years and I hated being broke. It kills me. I'm a money maker that tried to be legit and it was hard with all the shit that had happened to me.

Damn…could it get any worse?

Yes. It can. It can always be worse. You have to sometimes think about what's positive in your life. I just couldn't do that. I felt like a broken down pimp. I had once had so much in my life. I did gangster ass shit and now I was at the bottom because a White boy snitched and a Mexican businessman played me.

Chapter 14

The next twenty-four hours would be a blur. If I didn't have the police report to help me out, I wouldn't even remember how the next couple of days played out. I woke up early on December 21, 2012 very depressed, but I had to push myself and get out of the house. Who knew what I could stumble on. I've pulled bitches at gas stations, Walgreens, CVSs, bars, parks and all over, so I shaved and used some Magic Shave to make my bald head gleam. I showered and threw on black True Religion jeans, all black Jordan 4s, a black thermal with a button up black True Religion sweater hoodie combo. I had on black and gray blinged out rosary beads, my Ax watch and some platinum studs.

I had $400 in cash and some work. I jumped in the Audi A6. I needed a car wash first and to gas up. It wasn't even noon yet, but I thought I would grab a vodka and tonic water. By 1:00 pm, I had a little buzz, but nothing crazy. I went to play a couple of games of pool; by then, it was 4:00 pm and I hadn't stopped drinking vodka and tonic water, nor did I eat anything. It was time to get some bud for later. I stopped at the weed man's spot, smoked a blunt, drank a forty ounce of Old English and grabbed a gram of some killer ass shit. I'm not sure what it was, but it was stinking up the car. I had to double bag it.

By the time, I left the weed man; it was 6:00 pm. I had been drinking seven hours and didn't feel drunk yet. My homegirl called...she wanted to grab something off me and to go play pool at another spot. I stopped by her house and drank another forty ounce and smoked a little personal blunt while she was in the bathroom getting ready and getting high. I'm pretty sure she was shooting up in the bathroom. She was a pretty White girl; just a little too skinny for me and she loved White boys, so we were just friends. But I would have hit it if she would have given me the chance.

By the time she was ready, it was 8:00 pm. I had been drinking all day and had a nice buzz going on. We hit the pool hall and it was on. The bartender was hooking me up. I was in a zone. My boy, Gary, stopped by with a chick he was fucking, so spending time with them meant that I drank even more. I was lit by that time. The White girl I was with left and I didn't even realize it. Later she told me that she had told me she was leaving, but I was so drunk at that time that I don't remember that conversation.

I ended up talking some chick's ear off for a couple of hours, and then I got her number and decided to leave. It was midnight by that time. I had been drinking for thirteen hours. I stopped at a 7 Eleven for gas and a couple of hot dogs to sober up. I had some crackhead pump my gas for a couple of bucks while I ate one of the hot dogs.

At that point, I knew I shouldn't have been driving, but I had been drunker before in my life. I just needed to make it back to my mom's crib. She lived where there were dark black roads and I even had to drive by a police station. There also weren't any Blacks where she lived, so I was taking a big chance driving in the condition I was in. I put a Max B and French Montana CD on and rolled out. I sparked up a Black & Mild and was on my way.

I was driving slow, but I was lite. I was about half a mile from my mom's house and a cop pulled up on me. I took a left on to the road off of my mom's road and the cop followed me. I knew I was getting pulled over. He turned on his lights. I pulled over, took a swig of mouthwash and got my license and temporary registration ready. He came up to the window and I rolled it down and passed him the documents. Normally, I would have snapped out of it just from being drunk with a cop there, but I was too far gone for that. I was stuttering my words, telling the cop that I just wanted to get home and eat my hot dog. I was looking for something in my car while talking to the cop, and I am not even sure what I was looking for. Probably a Black & Mild. I don't know. When he asked me to step out of the car, I blacked out.

All I remember saying is, "NO!"

Then I remember him saying, "Don't put the car in drive!"

Too late. I was off…all the while, trying to make a phone call. I'm not sure who I was calling. Soon the car that sat on 19's in the back and 17's in the front – the Audi A6 – sat on an incline and started to spin out on the wet December roads. About 100 feet from my mom's house and 100 feet from where I got pulled over…I ended up on top of a rock with guns pulled out and pointed at me.

FREEZE, is all I heard from every direction.

I tried to get out of the car, but my doors were pinned. So when the cops said, "Don't go anywhere," I simply answered, "I'm stuck. Get me out of this car!"

They dragged me out with my pants falling off. *What the fuck have I done?* I thought my car was totaled and that I was going Upstate.

When they took me to the police station, I blacked out again and told the arresting officer that I was going to fuck his wife and his girlfriend. I guess he was cheating. *Ha ha!* Even drunk, I had a little respect so I didn't want to talk about his momma. He wanted me to sign some papers and I had to piss, so I took the paper, wiped it on my balls, then on my ass and pissed on it. I was fucked up. I told the cops that my watch cost more than a week of their pay and that my jeans cost $350. I was bugging I told them I was on probation and I was going to jail anyway so I didn't give a fuck. Then I got butt ass naked. When they tried to take my picture showing my Handle Ur Biz tattoo on my forearms, I was definitely bugging out.

After my outbursts, I finally fell asleep and woke up about a half an hour later. I asked the cop what I was charged with and he said, "DWI, Disobeying an Officer, and Criminal Mischief." Then he added that they had found drugs on the side of the road.

I said, "That shit ain't mine! They didn't see how it got there, so they can't charge me with it. That shit wasn't mine! I'm sticking to that shit!"

The cop said, "Your bail is $40 and you can take it out of the $480 that you have. I have been telling you that for the last hour now."

I cleaned up the piss and apologized for my actions. I didn't want to call my mom. I don't know why, but I called Raquel even though I hadn't spoken to her in over a year. She didn't answer and

I told the cop that she was probably getting Vampire fucked. I guess I was still a little drunk.

Finally, I called my mom, and as usual…she was always there to save the day at 2:30 am on December 22, 2012.

What had I done?

I got back to the house, fell asleep. When I woke up, I called about my car. Damn…$300 for a tow, no work and $100 to my name. It wasn't looking good. I had to call my PO the next morning because the cops had already called so I had a lot of explaining to do. When my car arrived, it wasn't that bad after all. It wasn't totaled and was actually drivable. I later had one of my boys' father fix it; $400 with paint. Anywhere else it would have been $2,000 easy. He had done body work on a lot of my cars in the past. It's always good to know someone in the biz.

It didn't hit me until later that day how much I had fucked up. I was sure to get my probation violated after that little stunt. *Would I miss Christmas and New Years? What have I done?*

I slept for two days before my mother came in the room and said, "Get your punk ass up!"

She was right. I must have hit the steering wheel because I had a black eye. I was at my worst. I thought I was in a depression before, but now it was really bad! While most people were getting ready for Christmas, I was getting ready for my PO and a violation.

My PO must have been busy, because I didn't hear from him till January 3rd. He told me to come in a week later. I was sure I was going to jail. I fucked the two bitches I was fucking with over that week and I got drunk. I tried to tell myself, *Fuck It! It will just max out my probation for nine months,* but my lawyer informed me that I still had that three to five years over my head and that the judge could give me five fucking years.

Damn…What the fuck have I done?

I went to see my PO on January 10th. He told me that he wasn't violating me yet, but he had applied for a warrant for my arrest. He said that when it came, I should turn myself in and I would get a violation hearing.

I was ready to go to jail that day! I left there and because of all the alcohol I had drank the night before and the stress I was under, I threw up everywhere. When I got home, the warrant was in the mail.

I guess this is my last night...again. I said to myself. Then I got drunk again, got some head and by the time the Sheriff called, I was ready to turn myself in. The Sheriff said that if I turned myself in early enough, I would have court the next morning, so that is exactly what I did. I spent the night in jail thinking that I would be there for a while. When I went to court the next day, the prosecutor wanted $40,000 bail and said that I was a menace to society.

I thought, *First, $40,000...Bitch, you CRAY, and second...menace to society? Bitch, I ain't o dog!*

I cut her a look that even the bitch that was typing the hearing looked back at me like, *You better straighten your face.* I was looking all crazy. The judge looked over my paperwork and gave me another $40 bail. I was free again. But for how long? The judge added that I would get a violation hearing to determine the outcome.

Chapter 15

Over the next month, I found a job and kept in touch with my PO trying to stay on his good side. I thought that maybe I could just max out in jail and be out in nine months. I wasn't sure how it worked. After a week or so out on bail, I got my violation hearing date; February 7, 2013…my fucking birthday! *What the fuck!* I also had court for the DWI on February 21st, so it was going to be a long month. I cut all of the bitches I was fucking off, and spent the rest of my free time working, stressing and dealing with the other bitch that I knew wouldn't last through my bid. I was going to keep her till February 6th and cut her bitch ass off. If I was going to be locked up for the next nine months, the last thing I needed was some bitch that wasn't totally down for me; you dig?

Well, February 6th came quick and like I said, I cut that punk bitch off in my mom's driveway, but not before I tried to get some ass. She wouldn't give it up so it made it that much easier to dump her. She shed one tear and was on her way.

Bitch, I knew you weren't down!

I don't blame her. I hadn't been myself since all of this shit happened.

February 7th came…my thirty-fifth birthday. My mom and I showed up for court. I had faith on the way there, but once I saw my PO's face, I knew I was going to jail. He told me that he hadn't even read the police report yet, but that if he had, he would have placed a hold on me then.

I was being offered either six months and I would be out in four but still on probation for four months, or one year and I'd be out in eight months.

No probation.

Fuck it…I'd take the year.

The judge wanted to send my ass Upstate, but chose to go with my Probation Officer and the Prosecutor's decision. I smiled to my mom sitting in the front row and blew her a kiss. It hurt to see her crying. I was handcuffed, sentenced to twelve months; one year in the county house of correction.

I sat in the holding tank for about an hour and when the Sheriff came to bring me to the jail, we drove by where my mom was parked and her car was still there. I knew she couldn't drive because she had been crying too much. It killed me.

I knew I had to get my mind right though. I thought to myself that I would workout hard, read more books and maybe write a book of my own. I had to stay positive.

*****

So much has happened over the last five months. I have eighty nine days and a wake up left. I'm not sure what's going to happen over the next eighty-nine days or whenever I walk out of here. I just know it's IN GOD'S HANDS.

To be continued...

Chronicles of A Hustler II

By Tarik Adams

A.K.A. Mr. Handle Ur Biz

Chapter 1

When I walked into Brentwood County Jail on February 7, 2013 – my thirty-fifth birthday, I was actually in good spirits. For one, I had been through the process before; and for two, I wasn't going to let anyone break me down on my birthday. It was kind of like the jail through a party for me because when I arrived in booking, Sergeant King was there to greet me.

"Oh, Mr. Adams, how long do we have the pleasure of your company this time?"

"I'm here for the long run this time; one year, or eight months with good time behavior."

Then I asked him how I could move straight to G Block. At this jail, they have two sentenced blocks: F and G; with G being the working block with a lot more privileges. In G Block, the inmates are out all day and only locked down from 7:30 am to 8:30 am and again at 2:30 pm to 3:30 pm for a shift change. Then they are locked down at 10:00 pm for the night. There is also coffee, a microwave, washer and dryer, extra trays of food, and it's just an all-around easier block to live on. But it's also a working block, so you have to have a job. On the bad side, it's also a P.C. Block – Protective Custody block, with skinners, rats and gays.

If I am going to be here for a year or even eight months, I wanted it to be the easiest time possible. Shit…I'd be working most of the time anyway, and I know how to do time, so I'd be keeping to myself. I came in alone and I'll be leaving alone.

As I was asking about G Block, the Sergeant pointed to Corporal Voight, who also remembered me. The Sergeant told me that Voight was the new Classification Officer, so he was the one in charge of assigning the inmates to the different blocks. When I last left here, Corporal Voight was just a CO (Correctional Officer) and he was always at the medical cart hitting on the nurses. He was cool as a CO, but those stripes could go to a mutherfucker's head real quick. We will see though!

He said, "I will see what I can do, but for now you will go to F Block."

Now F Block didn't have shit. You barely got hot water to make your (batch) to cook soups and other food. You definitely didn't have coffee and extra trays. The block was split up in two tiers: upper and lower. The lower tier was served breakfast at 7:00 am inside the cell along with the upper tier, except that the lower tier got let out at 9:30 am, lunch at noon in the F dining area and then locked back up at 2:30 pm for the rest of the day. You had to start on the bottom tier until you were classified, which took anywhere from two to five days. So that was twenty-three hours of lock down with only one hour out.top tier was almost like a hotel with breakfast and lunch brought to your cell and then you got out from 3:00 pm to 10:00 pm at night.

I still had the booking process to finish: finger printing, picture, and change into my greens. I had come in with $200 so that I could make phone calls and get some canteen/commissary. You wouldn't think that you would need money in jail; at least I didn't think that before I went in the first time. But it comes in handy. The three meals they feed you are not enough; especially for a grown man weighing over 200 pounds. Shit...even the eighteen year old boys in here kill the trays and are looking for more. Plus, your last meal is served at 5:00 pm, so that makes for a long, hungry night. Also, your hygiene products are very important. Being Black, lotion is a necessity. You also have to get your own soap unless you are going to use the State soap, which will have you dry and itching. Deodorant is a must too; even though it's a cheap brand that you could find at any local dollar store. In jail, you end up paying triple the amount for it, but it's better than the State stuff, if you're lucky enough to even get that.

You can also buy toothpaste and one, if not the most important, thing that you need is a pair of shower shoes. Most likely, I will know someone on the blocks, so I'd be all set with some of the stuff.

I was right. Before I even left booking, a CO that I knew slipped me a cup, a bowl, and shower shoes. Most COs are fucking losers, but every once in a blue moon, there's a cool one that doesn't bring his outside problems into work with him and doesn't let his little bit of power go to his head. I swear...most of them were picked on in school. They walk around knowing that if they get punched in their face, it's a three to seven years added on an inmate's sentence. I know that in prisons where motherfuckers are serving life, they don't pull that same shit on them. What does a prisoner serving life have to lose?

Once I arrived at the block, I made a quick glance around, knowing some of those dudes might be there with me for the next eight months to a year. I was also trying to show those motherfuckers that I wasn't no punk. One of the first people that I noticed, I thought he was a crazy looking Puerto Rican with a tat on his head and one on his neck that said, People = Shit. I soon found out that I was wrong and he wasn't Puerto Rican, he was a Guinea from New York named Paulie V. Over the next seven months, I grew very close to Paulie. You will end up hearing a lot more about him during my bid.

The next person to catch my eye was a sight that no one could have missed. He was a 6'5", 380 pound Black dude from Lawrence, Mass that could have went Pro, but drugs had fucked up his life. He was a crackhead who was simply known as Heavy. He had one of the craziest looks I had ever seen, with a lazy eye like that dude, Debo from the movie, Friday. I also found out that he was just like Debo when he was on the streets of Lawrence; when on his crack binges he would just take shit!

He stared me down; I never lost eye contact with that dude. I knew right then and there that he was going to be a problem. I wasn't worried though; even though I hadn't worked out in a while, my hands were always nice. I could hold my own; plus, when I lived in Upstate, New York, I had trained in boxing for a year before I moved back to Mass. Shit…if I got fucked up, he was going to catch a couple of his own, believe that. I wasn't too worried because I wasn't going to be in general population for at least three to five days and I'd be on bottom tier and he was on top tier, so it would be at least two weeks before we met up and I wasn't going to stress that.

I went to my cell, which was number eight with my bed role, toilet paper and toothbrush and made my mat up, tying the end of the sheets on each end so the green alligator (the mat) wouldn't touch my body. Then I banged out 100 pushups that seemed like 1,000. I was out of shape bad; but I had another eight months to get it back. Well, eight months if I didn't lose my good time.

The first person to come to my cell was a young boy asking me if I had brought anything "in" with me. A lot of inmates knowing that they are about to do time, will smuggle drugs in their jail purse, jail wallet or even in their butt, to get set up with mad canteen when they get there or to kick a habit, and I brought money in with me to put on my books, so there was no need. Plus, I wasn't stupid, that was another charge in itself for introducing drugs to a facility and would get an additional three to seven years. I wanted to be out of that bitch, not get more time.

"Naw, I didn't bring anything," I told the young boy.

"Ok. Don't worry about the dude, Heavy…he just be trying to punk people."

"Well, I'm no punk."

"Well, I am," the White boy said with a southern twang.

I had noticed a little bit in the way he talked, but I just thought he was soft and young, but then I realized what he was doing. He was hitting on me.

"You rainbow chasing flying unicorn, get your punk ass away from my cell!"

He stormed off mumbling, "You don't have to be so mean."

I would later find out they called him Fruit Punch and he had a twin brother that they called Super Punch because when he was at his jail job in the kitchen, he had punched a hot pot of mashed potatoes. He was just a wild young White boy like that who was always doing some dumb shit. I would run into so many clowns like this during my bid…it was crazy.

The second person to come to my cell was the dude, Paulie V. Now, right away, I could tell that dude was a solid motherfucker.

He said, "What did that faggot want?"

I laughed and said, "You already know; my G trying to see if I had brought something in."

He laughed and you could tell he was a street-smart dude from New York because it was as if he already knew the answer because he never asked if I did. He was in for fake scripts of Perk 30's, where he had passed over 100 all over New England and only got caught for a handful of them. He was serving a year also. He got there about a month before me, so we would be leaving around the same time.

"Do you read?"

"Yeah, I do."

"I have been collecting all the hood books that I could since I arrived. I'll drop some off."

And that's exactly what he did, and just in the nick of time because that night, he got moved to G Block and it would be almost a month before I got to see him again.

I was in heaven. He dropped off Deadly Reigns by Teri Woods, which was a tease because it was only the first book. He also dropped of Dutch I, II and III by Teri Woods which I already had read, but I had wanted to read again. There was also True to the Game I, II and III. I already had read them also, but a good book can always be read twice. There was also Death Around the Corner by C-Murder, Master P's brother who had written the book while he was locked up. He also gave me The Godfather which I thought that the book was better than the movie. I was never able to finish the movie, but I crushed the book in a week.

There was also Trust No Man 1, 2, and 3 which was written by a dude name Cash that had been locked up for seventeen years and Final Education of a Felon by Edward Bunker, also a very good book.

Just by the books he chose to give me, I knew that and Paulie V. and I were on the same page. The next three days locked in the cell for twenty-three hours a day with one hour out flew by so quickly. I read and did push-ups. When I finally did see the Classification Officer – CPL Voight – he told me I would have a job soon and would move to G Block. He also told me I could be moved to the top tier within a couple of days. I really didn't care; I had a cell to myself and plenty of books...so I was good. My pushups were going up and I started to shadow box, so I was feeling great. The day after I was put in population, we were locked down for twenty-three hours because people were popping milk carts and kicking their doors till 3:00 am. It didn't bother me though. I'd rather do cell time than fuck with the cornballs in this jail. Most of them were drug addicts and I didn't have any drugs to sell, so there was nothing for us to talk about. Their stories were always the same...they couldn't wait to get out and get high and how many drugs they had done in their life.

My first Bunkie came on my sixth day. He was a Spanish dude from Lawrence, Mass named Antonio. He was a cool guy even though he was also a dope fiend in for boosting shit from Kmart. Kmart? Really? Shit...he deserved to be locked up. He could have stolen from anywhere...Home Depot, Best Buy, and Target...anywhere. But Kmart? I didn't even know they still had them.

He had done Mad time before, but that was before he had kids, so this time was hard for him. He was a stress box. He missed his kids, so he was constantly talking about how he had to get out of here. It was funny to me because he only had 45 days left. I had 240 days left.

The next couple of days, I spent reading, getting my cell workout in and playing cards with my Bunkie and a lot of sleep. You wouldn't imagine how much sleep you get in jail. There's not much else to do. Read, eat, workout, eat again, sleep, cards, eat, read some more and sleep…it's the same thing every day unless something happens on the block. I didn't have to wait long. There's always some fool that forgets that they are in jail and sometimes it's like they get stupider right before they are about to leave. Just like the White boy they called Lurch. I'm not sure of his real name, but they called him Lurch because of his 6'6" frame and his goofy ass walk.

Within my first week, he was caught making hooch, which is home brewed alcohol made in jail by adding fruit, juice, sugar and letting it sit. These White boys will do anything to get fucked up. His dumb ass was supposed to leave in three days. He could have went to a bar and been drinking anything he wanted if he just waited three days. I just don't understand motherfuckers. You can see why he is in jail; he is dumber than a box of rocks. He might hurt himself on the streets.

Just in case you have never been locked up in the belly of the beast, let me tell you some of the shit you have to deal with on a daily, hourly, even a minute by minute bases. First are the people:

scrams, bugs, addicts, skinners, rippers, rats, queens, punks, racists, clowns, corns and straight bitch ass niggas. Not only are they on the tier with you, but you had to eat with them, bunk with them, breathe the same air as them, and smell their funk. It's crazy because these are people that you would never even look twice at on the street and you have to see them every day. After a while, everything they do gets under your skin; their face, walk, speech, swag, the way they eat. Everything about these punk ass bitches will make you want to smack the taste out of their mouth. They come in all sizes, shapes, colors, nationalities, ages, and the longer you are around them sharing the same air, the more it makes you realize how much you hate those motherfuckers.

Here are some examples: first you have dudes like Frankie the Phone. He's called that because as we would say on the inside, he is doing a phone bid, always on the phone crying to his bitch about some shit. There's one thing you need to learn about jail and that is you leave the streets on the streets. There's nothing you can do about that shit. The worst is to watch a grown man crying over some bitch that is most likely fucking someone else. Crying because she didn't answer the call and then complaining to anyone that will listen about her. He is such a sucker-for-love ass dude that he has work release where he gets to leave the jail and work a job and receive a check for $400, which the moment he gets it, he sends all of it to her. That leaves him with nothing for his canteen. All for a woman, that will most definitely leave him a week before he gets out.

Frankie the Phone wouldn't be the first to get beat like that; a Black dude whose last name was Temple who was just here…got it the worst. He was serving twelve months, no good time; 365 days because he caught a domestic and stalking charge on his wife who did not talk to him for his first six months locked up. But as soon as he got the work release, she happened to try to work things out with him. She pimped his ass over the next six months. She received over $7,000 from him and being a sucker for love…you don't see the signs right in front of you. For days, she wouldn't answer the phone and he was sending every dime and sometimes keeping $20 for calls and a couple of soups.

He would spend his time after breakfast asking for people's extra bread. Sometimes he would have a loaf worth. I'm not sure what he was doing with it. Eating bread sandwiches? What topped it all off was that she would show up to the visits every once in a while she did that to make sure she could keep her cash cow. Each time she came, she had on new kicks and new gear, while that fool was in here working sixty hour weeks, eating bread sandwiches and State food. Not to mention the fact that he could have used the money; he was missing his whole upper front row of teeth at only thirty-eight years old. I kind of felt bad for the brother. Everyone on the block that had any common sense knew what was to come and when it did, I wasn't surprised.

Two week before he was to leave, it was on. She caused a fight over some stupid old shit. He sent one more check and she filed for a restraining order on him and got her number blocked. You should have seen this fool when he realized what was happening, but he didn't stop there. He continued to call her from a phone he had at work. He is lucky he didn't catch another charge with his stupid Black ass. You would think that after 365 days in jail, he would have learned his lesson. She called the jail and told them that he must have had a phone at his job and he was still calling. The jail Lieutenant and a couple of COs went the next day, found the phone at his job, and lugged his Black butt back to jail. He went to F Block and spent the last fourteen days on twenty-hour lock down. He received his last check of $345, and his dumb, broke, sucker-for-love ass was released from jail on time. Hopefully, he didn't go stalk his $7,000 former wife and catch another charge.

That's just a few examples of the people in jail. I'll talk more about them later. I could go on for days about those fools!

Chapter 2

After about two weeks or a little less, I was moved to the top tier. I had been working out every day since I landed back in jail, doing a couple hundred pushups a day and shadow boxing. I was already down like fifteen pounds and feeling good. If Heavy wanted a piece of this, he was going to have to pack a lunch because it was going to be a long day, which he would soon find out.

I kept my distance for the first day, but when called to sit down with him and a couple of people for a game of Spades, I said, "Yes." Rather than trying to avoid the problem, I sat down with it. I think the fact that we were the only two Blacks on the block and Heavy wanted to run it, he figured he would take me out first. I had no desire to run the block. Shit…I was trying to go to another block anyway. If he would have talked to me, we could have worked together.

I knew there was a problem right away. It was my deal and he accused me of dealing from the bottom of the deck. The argument got heated real quickly; before I knew it, we were walking toward the laundry room. My blood was pumping fast. The other two players were to be lookouts. There was only one CO on duty, so this could be going on for a while. No one was going to break this shit up!

When we walked in the laundry room, I started my little boxer bounce that has gotten me out of many fights before; but it also loosened up my legs. I was ready. That fool must have thought I was going to try to talk that shit out. Fuck that! I had some stress to release and he was perfect to release it on.

He barked out, "Fuck You" at me and then charged me with his head down like a linebacker. I came up with my right knee flush on his chin. He backed up about four feet and shook it off. I could feel my knee buckle when I put it back down. I bounced it off and waited for him to charge again. He must have learned his lesson because the second time he came at me, his head was slightly higher. I threw a straight left and an overhand right; connecting right on his nose. I finished it off with a left hook.

Bang! Bang! Bang!

Once again he backed up about four steps and shook it off; but his eyes were blurry with tears. I knew that he felt those last three punches. I knew that I couldn't get close to him. If he got ahold of me, it was over. He outweighed me by 100 pounds. When he came at me again, I stepped to the right; just out of his reach and timed it just right with a vicious overhand right to his jaw. He stopped dead in his tracks and landed on his knees first, and then his face, with his feet to the sky. He was snoring like a baby. I didn't even miss my stride as I walked out of the laundry room with the two lookouts following me. As they went their separate ways, I went straight to my cell and about a half hour later, I could hear the COs rushing to the laundry room.

I'll give it to Heavy, he was a solid dude. He didn't snitch, he told the guards that he fell, which made me have respect for him. The ass whipping must have done the same for him because months later, when he was moved to my new block, we became cool.

That night, I was moved while he was in the nurses' office. Corporal Voight had found a job for me working third shift maintenance. He explained it wasn't the best job, but it got me to

G Block like I wanted. He told me that once a better job came up, that I could have it. It was probably for the best that I moved that night. It gave Heavy and I time to cool down.

I was trying to get work release, so I had sent a motion to the Court and then fell asleep thinking about what I would do with the money I would leave jail with. I wanted to take the Audi and drive across country to Arizona so bad. My hopes were high and it gave me something to look forward to. No matter what…I was going to keep up with my workouts. My plan was to come out of jail at 205 or 210 and able to do 1,000 pushups in two hours. I was already down twenty or so pounds that first month and I was banging out 300 pushups like it was nothing.

Having been so out of shape when I first came in at 265 and going so hard with my old ass, I started to get little injuries and needed to take a couple of days off between workouts. First it was my shoulder, and then it was my biceps. The days off in between gave me a lot of time to think about my life and how time flies. When you're younger, you want to be older and when you are older, you want to be younger; it's crazy how life works. OGs say, "If I knew then what I know now." I was feeling the same way. I don't have many regrets, but in anyone's life, there's always going to be things that they wished they did differently.

The third shift job I was working was for the birds, but if I wanted work release or a better job, I would have to stick with it, and boy did it suck! You worked seven days a week from 11:00 pm to 4:00, 5:00 or 6:00 in the morning. You swept and mopped the whole jail, you cleaned the CO's lounge and bathrooms, took out all the trash for the whole building and four times a month you had to buff the floors. On top of all that other shit, you also had to clean booking and the female tanks every night and no there were no females in the tanks at the time. The job sucked and once you finally did fall asleep, you were awakened by a loud inmate or an even louder CO.

The job was starting to fuck with me. I was getting grumpier by the day, but the time was flying by because when you were not working, you were sleeping. Two weeks passed before I even noticed it. I was a month into my bid. Only seven months to go.

When I was awake, me and my new-found brother, Paulie V, spent

time playing Spades and telling stories. Over the next couple of

months, you rarely saw one of us without the other unless we were

asleep or working.

The first month locked up, I received a card from my Auntie

Fay. Now my Aunt was a strong lady that had been through a lot in

her life. She was my mother's sister. She promised to send me at

least $10 bucks a month out of her SSI check, which she did; all

except for one month because she was known to go into a store and

start scratching Lotto tickets, thinking that she was going to win.

Well, she didn't that month, and she spent the $10 plus her money

for her meds. It was always funny to me that she did that. Her

Lotto addiction was always a better addiction than the drugs which

she had fought for many years. She was now five years clean,

which I was very proud of her for. She watched me grow into the

man I had become. It was her house that I would stay at when my mom would disappear for a week or so at a time when I was young.

My Aunt treated me like more of a son than a nephew. One of her biggest problems though, was the men that she chose. Once, one of her lovers tried to shot her while she was pregnant. She blocked the shot, holding her hand up and she now carries a fat finger for it that is slightly noticeable. Even with all of these types of things happening in her life, she stayed strong and was a single mother of three, that she did her best to keep a roof over their head and a fourth child if you wanted to count me because I spent a good amount of my youth there. Every once in a while, she would slip up with her drug addiction, but mainly, it was the punk ass man she fell in love with that over the years would spend up the Christmas money that she had saved, and days before Christmas, I would have to give up a couple of my presents so that my cousins had something.

My Aunt Fay is one of the strongest women that I have ever met. Besides growing up broke and struggling with her own addictions and heartbreak, she always kept going on with her life. Many weaker people would have tried to take their own life years ago, but not my aunt. She would always try to move forward with her life, no matter what she went through. Her strength – that also runs through my blood – was one of the things that kept me going through my bid. When you are locked up, it seems like everyone forgets about you and my aunt had my back since I was born. She was still in my corner for me at that age of thirty-five and I will always love and respect her for that. This book is for a lot of people in my life that have believed in me. Auntie Fay Thomas…this is for you. Even if it never gets published, I'm sure she will be one of the few that read it.

People don't realize what a simple letter can do for a person locked up. It could brighten your day up or ruin your day; but it is always nice to know someone on the outside is thinking about you.

*****

Time was flying with the new job, but it was stressful. You lived with the person you worked with. That meant you spent a lot of time with someone that you pretty much just met. I'm not sure of the science behind that when the jail set it up. Maybe because you are on the same schedule, they believe it will help you; or maybe they were trying to test your patience, knowing that the world is not going to be easy and if you don't kill a person that you barely know after spending damn near every minute together, then you are one step closer to being able to deal with life. When I say, damn near every minute, I mean every minute. It seems like the only time you are separated is when you are in the shower. More than likely, you sleep at the same time, you tend to eat at the same time, and then you have to work all night together, seven days a week. After a couple of weeks of that, it's very hard to get along with anyone.

My Bunkie was a drug addict that was doing time for burglary/robbery and he spent a lot of time in and out of jail. He had just left one jail after doing nine months. He was free for a month and now was serving another eight months. He had two years' probation with a three to seven year sentence over his head

Upstate. If he fucked up, and I'm pretty sure he will because he was an addict and even with the last year and a half lost to jail, he still wanted to go out and get high. He had two kids, and sometimes he would talk about getting out and having a normal life with his kids; but that would quickly fade and he would start talking about the streets and getting high again.

I have no kids, and my main love is money. I drank, but I can stop for a period of time to try to get my life on point. He and I didn't have much in common and it started to show. There were many points over the one month that I worked with him where I wanted to smack the shit out of him, but I held back. I was still trying for work release, which I had high hopes for, but it ended up getting denied. The judge wanted to give me more time, so he thought the sentence I got was light and wasn't going to approve of it. I wouldn't find that out until months later; instead, I figured if I do some of the programs that the jail offered, that might help my situation when I wrote a new motion a few months later. So I did the NA, AA, Bible study, choir, chapel anger management…you name it. I later found out it was all a waste of time, but I didn't know that so I kept the faith. Like I said, many times, everything happens for a reason.

After a month of living with and working with a person that I was starting to hate everything about and I mean everything: his hair, teeth, smile, voice, walk, jokes, smell and even the way he slept. It was all really starting to get bad. But then I got a new job and it was one of the best jobs you could get in jail other than work release where you made some real cash. I still got paid the buck a day, but it had so many other perks, and never in a million years would I guess that I would be working at a police department. Yes, I said a police department; the Raymond Police Department to be exact. I worked Monday through Thursday, which was perfect for me; not enough for me to hate the job, but just enough that after the three days off, I was ready to go back to work.

I only had to wash cars and they only had eight or so. On a Monday, I'd bang out most of them and only vacuum or touch up a few on the other days. It was an easy job. I would just sit in the

Sally Port (garage) and read and listen to an old radio they had. It didn't get the best stations, but it did the job.

Now, the perks weren't too bad. As many people who have been locked up know...getting out of the jail alone is a perk in itself, but I was also able to smoke a cig with the old maintenance guy named John who would throw me two cigs every day. Shout out to John. He was a cool old man. The dispatch lady also threw me four to six every other day and the other dispatch guy, Ed, bought me a pack of Black & Milds; all of which made my month. It's some of the simplest things that make a person in jail happy. The best perk of all that I received...the one that would make all inmates and convicts throw a thumbs up was that they let me order $20 of food from a sub place every day for lunch; steak tip dinners, steak and cheese, chicken parmesan dinners, pizza, Buffalo wings, and anything I wanted.

I was eating like a king; at least Monday through Thursday. Seeing that I was watching my weight, I had it down to a science. I'd order a steak tip salad and a side of grilled chicken. The grilled chicken came with eight chicken breasts, so I'd eat four of them, all the steak, and half of the big salad and save the rest for when I got to work the next day. Then on Thursdays, I'd have a chicken parmesan dinner with a side salad, and garlic bread. I had a Powerade with every meal. When you are locked up, some of the things you miss the most are food, pussy, family and of course...your freedom. I was getting a little food and freedom, so that was good enough.

Being on G Block, you were able to have touch visits. A lot of the inmates took advantage of it, but I had one visit which was my mom. It was nice, but I told her I'd see her when I got out. I've always been a momma's boy, so it was hard to watch her leave. That one visit affected me for a couple of days after it. I made up my mind then that I was going to do this bid...and I was going to do it without visits. I wrote letters and used the phone every once in a while; not much because they don't call it the stress box for nothing.

The phone really is a stress box. Hearing the simplest things on it can ruin your day. I once called my mom and when I asked what she was doing, she said she was cooking fried chicken, baked macaroni and cheese, collard greens and corn bread. Let me state for the record that I love my mom's cooking and that's one of my favorite meals that she makes. Just that one simple comment from her about what she was making had me salty for a couple of days. There are just some things that you don't want to hear about that are going on in the streets.

In another convo with her, she explained how my younger, twenty-five-year-old brother had been treating her. My blood was boiling, but there was nothing that I could do from here. I couldn't even call him because if I did and he turned into a telephone tough guy and tried to phone wrestle with me, there would be nothing I could do from a jail cell. That would only result in me taking it out on one of the bitch ass inmates and possibly catch another charge for assault. But trust and believe...he will feel my pain when I get out. Word is bond; so like I said…I stay away from the phone and stick to writing a few letters to keep in touch.

There are rules to this jail life like there are rules to the game of life. So far, I am doing ok with all of them. I have had my slipups, but doesn't everyone? My Police Department job was going ok. They put a new Bunkie in my cell that had a job at the Police Department too. I really didn't like that fool from the start. He was another addict. This jail has so many. He was serving fourteen months for passing fake prescriptions and had two and a half months left. We never really talked the first week in the cell, but one night he came back to work and wouldn't shut up. I could tell he was high on something. He later told me it was suboxone and that his girl was dropping them off at his police job. He had already told me too much. I was just wondering how many people he had told that information. I knew it wouldn't take long for him to get caught. He had promised a couple of people that he would bring some in, and when he didn't…it was easy to see that there were hard feelings by the other addicted ass inmates. No one wants to see you shine; especially when you are walking around the block all fucked up, rubbing it in their face and that is just what he was doing.

It only took another inmate – who he had promised to provide suboxone to – to get caught with some tobacco to rat him out. When my Bunkie came back from work, there was a piss test waiting for his dumb ass. He was dry tanked, where they keep you in a cell with no toilet flushes to see if you have a package stuck in your jail wallet, jail suitcase, jail purse, or your butt. He was lucky; he didn't have any; but he lost his job and was lugged back to F Block to spend half his days locked up. He lost ten days of good time and seven in the hole.

The hole is twenty-three hour lock up with one hour out to shower and work out. I'm not sure what he was thinking being that he was so close to getting out. He was also having sex with his girl. He had the best of both worlds possible being in jail; if only he could have shut his mouth.

At that point, I had been at my job for a month and it was starting to get old. The food was good and all, but I ate well on the streets. The cops were cool, but being around them all day was also getting old. I had over six months left and wasn't sure if I was going to be able to do this the rest of my bid. I was having doubts and the work release wasn't looking so good either. Like they say…you don't know what you have until it's gone.

Even the freedom of leaving the jail was a blessing and a curse. I was going to have to watch the summer pass me by. The leaves were starting to change on the trees and I could hear the cars passing by with music playing loudly. At least when you are locked up, you don't have freedom thrown in your face. That's all I could think about. I was battling with myself daily and not really realizing what a good thing I had while being in jail, but I would soon find out.

Chapter 3

My next cellmate was a fag. Really…he liked boys. He was a twenty-year-old kid that had been doing time since he was eighteen years old. He was also an addict while on the streets. I told him straight up that I didn't play that gay shit, so not to joke with me about it and to show me respect and I would do the same.

The first week went ok and then I came back from work and watched him walk by on the upper tier. His face was swollen like a bee had stung him and I could tell that something was going on on the block. People were buzzing all around my cell door. I stayed out of the cell and watched all the action. I could tell that those motherfuckers were all high. They had no swag at all with what they were doing. They had my cell door hot like it was the Carter in New Jack City. Dudes were sitting in front of the cell cleaning the railing and passing books in and out the cell. I finally went up to the room and it smelled like shit. I mean straight doo-doo, like he had been digging in his ass. He was definitely high. His face was swollen.

I asked him what was wrong with him and he didn't lie. He told me the truth right off the bat; knowing I could sense something was going on. That dumb ass motherfucker told me that he had broken into the evidence locker at the Police Department that he was working at and had brought back coke, heroin, pills, weed, a syringe and a hundred dollar bill. Seeing that his jail wallet was bigger than it normally should be, I could tell that he had done all of that in one trip.

The syringe alone had me thinking…damn, with the back of the police cars which they bring us in, being all plastic…all that shit just bouncing around in his butt was a shock to me.

He knew I didn't do drugs other than weed and maybe a perc here and there, but nothing ever going up my nose. He offered me some weed and a perc, and I had to say no.

With fourteen or sixteen other inmates walking around the block all fucked up, it was only a matter of time before the COs came rushing in. I'm glad I had said no, because what I didn't know was that his dumb ass had passed out in the back of the police car. He was nodding while he was being brought back to jail. That addicted ass kid couldn't even wait to bring it back, he had gotten high at the Police Station in the bathroom. I am not sure if he just had some balls on him, or if he was just that much of a fool ass addict. I was leaning toward him just being a fool ass addict.

When the cops dropped him off, they called back to the station trying to find out what was going on. They had found the door to the evidence room jimmied into with scratches from a screwdriver or something. Within two hours, they had the whole jail locked down and our whole block was searched. They brought all of us to the F Block dining area where you could see at least two to three people with the same nodding head that my Bunkie had. They pulled his dumb ass over to a separate table just to let him know that he had fucked up and that they were on to him. The other inmates gave him looks like, Damn, you're fucked. He was too stupid and high to realize the trouble he was in. Even the lieutenant was called in and came in his gym clothes. Shit…was going down hard.

They took him in the other room and we could hear the lieutenant yelling at him and then he was lead out in handcuffs, looking dumb and high at the same damn time. They next pulled in the biggest snitch on the block. He was also high as shit and the one that had snitched on my Bunkie. He did it because my cellmate had not given him any drugs. That dude must have sang like a fucking fat lady at the opera, because the next thing we knew, all the Police Department jobs were stopped and eleven people were called down to get a piss test.

I was called down because the gay guy was my cellmate. There was only one other person that was called down that didn't get high. The snitch had fingered everyone that got high thinking that he wouldn't get in trouble. Shit…it had worked for him before. Some of the people got off because they had started to drink water that same night and the jail had waited so long to perform the piss test. Seven people got lugged back to F Block;

one being a snitch and two work release people, which I couldn't understand why if they were getting a paycheck, why would they fuck that up to get high. They had the chance to leave jail with a couple thousand dollars in their pockets.

I was already missing my steak tips and my cigs and the freedom of being out the jail daily. What was I thinking? You don't realize what you got till it's gone. The third day after that, they raided the block again with dogs thinking that there was still drugs on the block. There was still some there, but the inmate had it in their jail wallets. They piss tested a couple more people. By then, it was too late. Their systems were clean. All Police Department jobs were off until further notice.

I was given a tier job of sweeping mopping, cleaning and passing out food about a week after the Police Department jobs were stopped. It was cool for a couple of days, but grew old real quick. Not being able to leave the block when I had previously been out the building four days a week and eating good and smoking good…was draining on me. I was back to the jail food like the rest of the scumbags.

After two weeks on the tier job, I asked that I be taken off. I wasn't liking it at all. It was like those motherfuckers were making the block even dirtier and complain about showers being cleaned and then blaming missing radios on me and the other tier workers. It turned out that two of the radios were missing and one was found on the basketball court. I was trying to stay under the radar, but it was impossible. That job brought me right on the front line. I couldn't stand it. All the Police Department workers came up with a clean piss, but we were all suffering from one stupid inmate. Inmates will always fuck up a good thing. Like they say, you give a nigga shit…he will fuck it up every time. When I talk about "niggas" in this incident, I am not talking about Black people; I'm talking about an ignorant person.

It would be over a month before the Police Departments went back to work like before. It was a big decision for the superintendent to make. That one inmate made the jail and the

Police Department look like fools. He lost all his good time: four months…with thirty days in the hole and he was waiting for more charges from the State and the Police Department. If it had of been my Black ass, I'm sure they would have thrown the book at me.

When the news did finally hit local paper, they dumbed down the whole situation and even told a couple of lies to make it not look so bad. You can never trust the news or the paper. There is truth in the saying, don't believe anything you hear and only half of what you see.

One good thing that happened while I was not working at the Police Department job was that I had more time to focus on the book. I was writing. It started out slow, but eventually, I was banging out a couple of pages at a time and stopping for a bit so that I didn't burn out. When I finally did go back to work, I was happy; which sounds strange…me, happy to go to a Police Department to work for a buck! But truth be told, I missed the steak tips and cigs and the fresh air. You get fresh air in jail when you get yard time, but you are surrounded by a fence and other inmates, so you don't feel as free as I did siting in the garage of a Police Department. I know that sounds stranger; but it is my reality.

I spent my time in the sally port of the police station thinking about where I would go next in my book and my life. I read a lot of different books and I wouldn't normally be interested in Helter Skelter, which was about Charles Manson's crazy ass. Even though he hated Blacks, I have to give it up to a pimp. I also read the book, The Town, which was a little different from the movie, but it was good. I liked it and my hometown was mentioned tons of times. Shout out to Malden, Mass. The Godfather was a good book. I never got to finish the movie. I found it boring, but the book…I couldn't put it down; that's the first time in my life where I could honestly say the book was better than the movie.

I had a lot of down time in the Sally Port. It gave me a lot of time to reflect on my life and the things I had done. I don't have many regrets; just that I wished I would have saved better. I'm not sure when in my life that went wrong. I was always one to have a stash or plenty of cars to sell, but catching a charge will do that to any young hustler. When you hustle, you are living in the moment and you never know what that moment will bring. It might even bring a drought, and that can really fuck a young hustler up.

Chapter 4

The game really changed after September 11th for anyone that really sold drugs. The prices went up and it was harder to find, seeing that the police stepped up their game everywhere; especially highway and air. Pounds of weed went from $600 to $1,200. Double in price. So did other drugs; but that part of the game is played...not lived. I was always living and not saving. I spent and never was as prepared as I thought I was. Life is funny in that way. Like I said, No regrets! I just would have done a couple of things a little differently.

While talking to the Lieutenant at the Police Station, I found out we were the same age. We talked about all the things that were going on when we were growing up, from Bo Jackson, Nintendo,

Jordans, Stater hats, Bel Biv Devo, Alyssa Milano, Cindy Crawford, Yo MTV Raps, Thunder Cats, Mc Hammer, to GI Joe. It made me feel a little old and wonder where my life went wrong. But then I quickly snapped out of that and just how I started my book…I understood.

First, the apple does not fall far from the tree. His dad, the Lieutenant that I was talking to, was a cop; mine was a pimp and drug dealer. He grew up around police. I grew up around pimps and hustlers. Yeah, I had a little bad luck, but I lived the life that he would never know. I fucked more girls in a summer than he had in his whole life. I've spent more money in a year than he had in ten. Damn…I've had more threesomes than he had sexual partners. My endless nights of breaking night (staying up all night) and partying with hoes…just period…the life I lived…I enjoyed it to the fullest. Maybe right now I'm not enjoying it seeing that I am sitting here writing this from a jail cell, but everything else was Gucci; the vacations, the Jag, BMW, Navigator, the strippers, and all those blunts and bottles of Hennessy.

I know what you are thinking…look were it all got you!

My answer to that is that I have memories of a lifetime. The things I've done and seen…guys only sit and dream about. They can lock up my body, but they will never be able to take away those memories. I truly have lived my life. At the age of twenty-one to thirty-one, I didn't work and I spent more money than most people do in their entire life. My life has been a vacation and a party. What's eight months to a year? Even with that down time…motherfuckers can't catch up to me. I've owned a biz and wrote this book.

I have maybe two more things in my life that I want to accomplish and I still have plenty of time to make those things happen. I get closer and closer to being a free man and the sky is the limit. I would like to believe that I won't commit any more crimes and that I will be good, but that would just be the jail and these bars talking. I'm going to be true to myself and my life. I have plans, but I had plans after my first little bid and it didn't work out as planned. But I'm still alive and have a lot left in me to keep it moving. My body is strong from all these pushups. My mind is strong from all these books. My soul has faith. Anything can happen when I leave this place. I won't have a lot of money and I'll have my Audi A6 with no license; but I'll have my freedom and my game. I've been broker with no shit. Box whips out of shape and made things happen, so I'm not worried at all. I'm a hustler to the death of me; legal or illegal, I'll make things happen.

*****

These last couple of pages might sound a little cocky, but it's not. I just believe in myself and what God has planned for me. It's no different than a born athlete believing in his skills every time he or she puts their feet on the court, baseball field, football field, golf course, etc.

I finished the first book in a month and a half and that was longer than I thought it would take, but with the bullshit that goes on the block every day, and the things that you have to deal with, it's understandable. Not to mention the fact that I didn't write every day. It's hard to stay motivated in this place, but I've done my best. I've worked out like a champ; I'm proud of what I've built and the books I've completed; also giving myself more knowledge.

Do the time; don't let the time do you. It's hard to stay with that mentality because your feelings about where you are go up and down. Some days you feel good and realize where you are at and that you're going to be free someday. Other days are rougher than others, where you can't see the light at the end of the tunnel and end up just staying in a bad place mentally. I'm not going to lie, I've had both good days and bad days and on those bad days, I eventually was able to snap myself out of it. Thank God, because if not, I can just imagine what might have happened.

Chapter 5

The days are starting to move on. The summer is passing me by. They can't stop time. I'm bunked up with my boy, Paulie V., but it's only a matter of time before they break us up. We have too much fun together after lock down playing cards and talking shit; and my boy Paulie has no inside voice. Other than one other person, he is the loudest on the block. It's funny though, he can't help it. The other loud person on the block is Heavy. He came on the block months ago and got work release rather quickly. It sucks though, because I would have made moves to change my life with the money he was getting; but since he is a crackhead, he already has plans on spending all of the money he makes on drugs. I can't hate on him for that though, it's his money. He worked for it, so he can spend it as he pleases; but it's not easy not to hate when someone has what you want and you know in your mind that you would have handled things differently. But it is what it is, and it's gonna be what it's gonna be.

Heavy and I had squashed our beef and have been cool over the last couple of months. He can still get on a brother's nerves real quick though. He is so ghetto that he can't help it. Every Black person knows someone like that. He can always find a way to ask someone for something, or to do something for him. It's real funny how he does it until he has the nerve to ask me…then he gets mad when he doesn't get the answer he wants. Even an ass whopping can't stop a pissing ass pit bull from pissing on the carpet; and that is just what Heavy is…a bad pit bull. He was able to save $4,000 from work release before he got fired from the job. That's $4,000 he will eventually spend on crack. What a waste; even more so because he gets out three weeks before I do. That money will all be long gone by the time I get out. No chance of me making any money off his crackhead ass. Besides, I'm still not sure which way I'm going to go with life when I leave this place.

The game on the streets right now is heroin. Every time I open the newspaper, that's all I see…people being arrested for possession of it, or sale of it. It is also the only drug that I have never sold. Heroin is a completely different game from coke, crack, weed, X, acid, and mushrooms. The people on heroin get sick, and the last thing they want to do is go to jail, so the snitch rate is very high in the game. Which reminds me…the dude Ryan – the one who snitched on me – was found dead a couple months into my bid. He snitched on someone so that he could continue to get high, and it ended up getting him killed. Karma is a bitch.

The whole house thing with Raquel of her taking me to court to get sole ownership of the house is not going in my favor. Not only is it hard for me to fight it from jail, but I set myself up for all of this a long time ago by living in the moment and being a fast moving drug dealer and pimp who was not totally planning for the future. I never saved the receipts for repairs and bills and remodeling the kitchen. I fucked up, and now she is going to get the house. In some ways, she deserves it, but in other ways…Damn! Touché.

Thoughts

July 13, 2013

My thoughts for the day

I was sitting and reminiscing about my grandparents. I was young when they both passed away, but I do have memories about them. Addiction runs in my family. They were both drinkers and smokers. As I remember, my grandmother drank very heavily and my grandad worked at a carwash and mainly drank after a hard day of work. I'll always remember the smell of their apartment in the projects. It was a mixture of cigarette smoke and spilled beer. Any person that has lived around that life can tell you the same.

From what I remember, they were both very nice and my granddad brought me and my other cousins to the car wash a good amount of time. I remember riding through it with the soapy water washing the car. I think all kids remember their first ride through a car wash. It was exciting as a kid to see all the different colors of bubbles and hear the water. It was even more special and memorable because it was with my granddad; it's a memory of him that I will always hold. RIP to my grandma and granddad.

My granddad lost his leg to Cancer and I'm pretty sure my grandmother lost hers life to old age and drinking. I'm not sure who died first. I would have to ask my mother that. What I do remember about my grandmother is that she was a very nice lady, but with her and my granddad being alcoholics, it depended on which time of the day you caught them and how much they had to drink. I get flashbacks of her yelling at people and I get flashbacks of her sleeping…passed out on the couch. I even have flashbacks of her smiling and being happy. The flashbacks of my grandad are slightly different. He reminds me of the old pimp, Fillmore Slim. He was tall, slim and a handsome man. I can't recall, but I never really remember him losing his temper and being mad.

Addiction has a different effect on me. I am a person that can drink for six months at a time, then snap out of it and not have a drink for over eight months, but I do know that I have the traits of an alcoholic or an addict. During the eight months that I am sober, I tell myself that I will not go back to day drinking or drinking every day. I will tell myself that I feel great being sober and working out and that I don't want to touch a drink ever again. I tell myself that and feel powerful and confident in myself. But once I have that first drink, all of that goes down the drain. Not right away, but maybe within a week or two. After that first drink, I'm right back at it; day drinking and drinking every day, not working out and being drunker than a skunk as they say, and I will stay like that for months. That behavior will go on until later when I wake up hungover and telling myself that it's time to stop again and then I'm on the wagon. It could be two weeks or two months or six months, it just depends on how I'm feeling at the time. What I do know is that I need to control it better than I have.

Chapter 6

Another day on the rock. People in jail can be such punks. I can't even imagine some of these punks on the street. This weekend, someone took the control for the TV and threw it away just to mess with the sixty-eight-year-old White man because he spends his day watching TV. He does not bother anyone. He sits in the same seat every day and those punks have shit to say about that. I was brought up to respect my elders. I don't see the gangster in trying to punk an old man. I know I have to do my own bid, but I can't help saying shit to people when I see things like this going on. Today was one of those days. Early this morning before chow started, one of the tier workers was really feeling himself. Tier worker is a job given out that has the inmate clean the block by mopping, sweeping, washing down tables, handing out food and things like that. The tier workers are able to stay out a little later than the other inmates so that they can clean and they are given other privileges such as more food and they pretty much get run of the block as inmates.

I had the job for a short time, but I didn't like cleaning up after sixty grown ass men. Some people can't handle the little bit of power that comes with the tier job. It goes to their heads and that was the case with this one guy who is a straight up bitch. He complains about damn near everything, and this particular morning, the old man grabbed his special sodium free meal from the bottom of the cart before the other inmate. When I worked the tier job, I made sure the older guys got their special meals first.

Well, the old man grabbed the wrong meal and I could hear the bitch ass tier worker complaining like a little bitch before the old man was able to return it. When the old man did return it, he apologized, "Sorry. I grabbed the wrong one," he said.

The bitch ass tier worker yelled and said, "That's why you need to wait in like everyone else!"

Mind you, he handed a younger inmate that he likes his special meal, but was treating the old man like shit. He is just a punk. A straight up punk.

I should have minded my business, but I barked at him, "Just give the old man his fuckin' food!"

"Why don't you mind your own business," the punk ass inmate yelled to me.

I almost lost all control and smacked the shit out of him, but quickly chilled out when I noticed he only said it because of the CO close by. I'm the fourth inmate in less than a week to get in an argument with that punk. The last inmate that argued with him got a slip dropped on him saying that he was bringing in shit from an outside trashcan that he had to clean for his jail job. I am pretty sure it was the punk as tier worker that did that shit. He is the worst kind of inmate; a punk, a snitch and a bully of old men that only gets loud in front of COs.

Frustration in jail can make even the best inmate "act out" which was the case with me one day with a young man named Randel. I had a slight resentment toward Randel ever since my first job as part of third shift maintenance. He was a float. A float is when the CO has no set block for the shift and does other jobs while on duty such as filling in for the COs while they are on break or, as in my case, watching inmates clean while they are in restricted areas.

On particular night, the topic of life was being thrown about between me and another inmate. He was thirty-five and had spent the majority of his life in and out of jail. Randel overheard our conversation and responded, "That's life."

I kept my mouth shut, but all I could think was, What the fuck does this twenty-two year old know about life? It's hard to respect those younger COs when your almost twice their age and out weight them by 100 pounds.

Earlier that morning after chow, Randel told all the inmates to lock in unless they were about to go to work, which I was about to do.

Without thinking, I looked him dead in the face and said, "Rub it on your chest," which in jail means, Fuck you.

I could tell he was heated when he said, "Serious?" and then he used my last name, which is what the COs called us by.

"Just kidding," I said.

He started walking toward me and said, "Get up!"

When I was halfway to him, my arm flexed. He reached out to grab my bicep, which he could barely grab half of it.

I pulled away and said, "Don't fucking snatch up on me."

He marched me to the hallway that led in and out of the cell block. It had a door on each side and there weren't any cameras in there, so we were pretty much blocked in. I could have stomped the shit out of him if I wanted to.

He then turned to me and said, "I don't mind if you say shit like that if we are alone, but in front of inmates, that disrespect ain't gone fly."

I couldn't respect his statement either. That was some bitch ass shit. I could say what I wanted to him as long as it wasn't in front of people?

I apologized anyway.

Then he looked at me and responded, "You're a retard."

I was heated. Not only did he grab on me, but he called me a retard.

I repeated what he said, "I'm a retard?" I stared him dead in the eye. He must have realized how heated I was and where we were…blocked in with no cameras.

"Yep," he said as he began going back in the area where we had just left.

It took everything in me not to punch him, or smack the back of his neck like the bitch he was. I walked in behind him and a couple of inmates that were waiting to go to work sat and laughed about what had happened before Randel and I walked out. I calmed down and realized it was fucked up what I had said to Randel. Inmates scream shit like that all day, but they do it from the privacy of their cells where it can be anonymous and the CO would never know who said it or where it came from.

Just to be a punk and act out, I guess…when I was leaving for work and when it was only me, Randel and another CO in the area, I said, "My bad."

Randel said, "We will let bygones be bygones."

I said, "That's cool, but you probably want to check your CO handbook; I don't think you can be grabbing all up on inmates like that if they are not being aggressive."

He said as he turned his back, "Well then…file a grievance."

While walking out, I said, "I don't need to. I just told you."

I know it killed him for me to get the last word. After I thought about it later, I knew I was wrong. Even smart people make bad decisions. I was mad at myself because since I am so close to leaving, there was no reason for me to be making bad decisions. It kind of scared me because there are too many choices that I need to make on the streets. One bad move and the next thing you know, you could be catching a case. With my record, one bad decision and I'll be doing a long bid. There are drug addicts in here that are afraid to go back on the streets because they know that they will fuck up again. The only time in their life that they are sober is when they are locked up. Me, on the other hand, my only fear is God – who is the ultimate judge, and being broke.

I'm not sure if I'm going to be good when I hit the streets. I want to, but this is the life I've lived since I was a young. Money, bitches and the game call me like crack did to Pookie in the movie, New Jack City. Like I said before, "It's all in God's hands." I don't know what He has planned for me. After spending that initial sixty days and the weekends in jail, I never thought that I'd be back in jail, but my saying has always been, Everything happens for a reason. If I never caught that initial bid, I would have never started writing, Chronicles of a Hustler.

Hustler's Intermission

Every once in a while during the book, rather than keeping with the story format, I'm going to talk about my thoughts. I've always had a hard time expressing my thoughts and feelings. Usually in a drunken ramble, I would try to explain them to an ex-girlfriend; which Raquel, Channa, Honey, and Stephian can attest to. They have heard them plenty of times; but over time, they probably never got the real point of what I was saying because being drunk, I would either never get to the end or to the point before switching subjects and rambling on about something else or repeating myself. Tonight as I sit in my cell sober, with it fresh on my mind, my thoughts are about what I'd like to call, Hustler's Nightmares. Any true hustler that has been in the life will know about them. They are dreams…no, nightmares that we have. Most of the time, a Hustler's nightmare centers around them running from the law or the cops have a warrant for your arrest. Some are in the form of you trying to hide or sell the last of your stash to flee the state or country. Or maybe the dream is about you robbing another drug dealer and you have their stash, and the law is after you and you have to hide the drugs or sell them quickly. In those nightmares, I would always hide them in dumb places like under a rock; and when I would go back, the stash is always gone and I am pissed off because I'm trying to figure out what I am going to do now that the money is gone and I have no way out.

In Hustler Nightmares, you are always running from the law and it feels like you're running for miles. With all the running and from the stress of trying not to get caught that you feel in your dream, which feels like reality, you wake up so drained, frustrated and exhausted.

*****

C.O.A.H.

July 10, 2013

One of my thoughts for the day is how hard it is to receive bad news in jail; or news of something that you have no power over and can't possibly fix from jail. When you are on the streets, you can call a lawyer or use the internet to find out information, but in jail, it's a lot harder to do simple things that normally you take for granted. There's so many ways to relieve your mind of simple stress on the streets; in jail, you have one or two options…work out or sleep. I have a third option now, which I feel blessed to have. Writing is now a way to relieve stress for me. I write about everything now. It makes the days and nights here easier to cope with. Behind bars, I let my pen deal with the frustration and anger that builds up inside my mind.

The issues of today overwhelm me. I knew the girl I owned the house with was hell bent on a war with me over the house, but she never ceases to amaze me. Even though I am over the initial shock, I'm still mad. I don't even want to writer her name down because it will just make me see red. That's why I called her, "the girl I owned the house with." She brings out that kind of anger in me. Dissociation is probably best.

Anyway…that girl had me served with paperwork today.

Bitch!

I had previously written a letter to the Court asking for more time to obtain legal representation in our case over the house. I used the fact that I was locked up as a mitigating circumstance for me being able to quickly find an attorney. I was given a deadline, which I met, but from the paperwork I was served with, I guess my letter was not in compliance with the Superior Court Pad Rules…whatever the fuck that means.

Damn…I hate this bitch.

Just like I asked the Court for time to get legal help, I quickly wrote a motion for a late entry and attached a copy of the first letter that I had sent. Then I decided to lie down and try to think more clearly about the options that I have…which aren't too many. The couple of options that I do have, I will go forward with them and hope for the best.

Everything happens for a reason.

It is what it is.

It's gonna be what it's gonna be.

It's in God's hands.

All of those were sayings that I have grown to use over the years. I have to live what I preach. I will encounter defeats, but I shall not be defeated.

I have a lot of mixed feelings about that house anyway. In some ways, I think that she deserves it because of all of the things that I put her through. In other ways, I think that she could have come at me in another way. I know that I will never know what was going through her head when she did it. I had lost her years ago. I also know that her actions are a direct result of mine toward her. So what can I say?

Whatever happens from the past days and the days that I have ahead of me, I will…Keep my feet planted on the ground and my head to the sky, like Lil Wayne said.

I'm Mr. Handle Ur Biz. All I can do is handle business; that's all I know till the death of me.

Chapter 7

So many thoughts go through your mind when you are locked up. Family…I wonder what my mother is doing at this moment. Is she happy? Is she driving? Is she thinking about me? Is she doing all three? There are so many possibilities when you are free. That brings me to my second thought. Freedom. Oh, what I'd do for it right now. What would I be doing right now if I was free? Who would I be with? What am I going to do on my first day out? That's one thing that I can plan and that I have the power to make happen. But then life will hit like a brick wall.

I don't want to get a head of myself though. On my first day out, I plan on hugging my mom so tight and then smoke a Black & Mild on the way home. When I get home, even though I plan on taking a shower before I leave the jail, I will take another one when I get home to wash the feel of jail off. I want to use my body wash that I miss so much. Then I will put on my street clothes, studs watch, Jordans, my cologne and after that's all done, I'll take a deep breath of freedom. Then I will sit on the couch with a cold glass of Hennessy and a Heineken while I watch Netflix with my mom.

Then I'll smoke a blunt and chill; filling my stomach with my mom's good cooking of eggplant, fried chicken, Spanish rice, baked mac and cheese, collard greens and anything else she prepares for me. After that, I'll take a nap and wake up to do it all over again. I know the food, alcohol and blunt will have me feeling nice. More of that and then more Netflix as I update my Facebook, Twitter, Instagram and set up some ass for my second day at home.

Sex, sex, and more sex while I sip, smoke and eat some more by the third day. It's about that time to make moves: money, money, and more money. How am I gonna get it will be a major thought, and how am I going to spend the rest of the year is another. What are my plans to bring in 2014 and make sure that it's better than 2013? That shouldn't be too hard seeing that I spent most of 2013 in jail.

I have plans, and I'll need to put them in motion; but at this point, this is all just thoughts and dreams because I am still sitting in jail for another seventy days or so.

*****

The days are starting to slow down the closer that I get to freedom. That's how it works sometimes. There was a little action on the block though. Heavy got in a beef with a racist ass White boy named Costello that I've wanted to smack for months. He is a PC from the state prison that walks around with those lightning bolt SS (which is the symbol for Skinheads) on his back. There are so many different stories of why he is here from the State prison and I'm not sure if any of them are true.

I had Heavy's back. We have become cool since our run in; besides, there are not too many of us brothers on this block, so we have to stick together. I'm not sure what the argument between Costello and Heavy was over, but I was still going to have Heavy's back against the racist ass White boy. For some reason, the dude tried to call Heavy out, but the CO that was on duty was one of those cool COs that opened the laundry room so it could all go down. Like a smart veteran CO, he took his break and had a rookie CO cover for him. It was a smart move. It covered his ass if anyone got beat to death…which almost happened.

After Costello called Heavy out, yard time was called, so Costello sat outside with seven or eight White boys trying to stare Heavy down hard, but Heavy didn't care. It was only me and my boy Paulie that had Heavy's back anyway. But that was more than enough. A lot of punk ass dudes in jail have mastered the art of getting out of fights by getting loud in front of COs, but Costello wasn't going to be so lucky this time. When yard ended, the CO opened the laundry room and took his break. Costello walked in first and Heavy followed. I blocked the door so if anyone was going to jump in, they had to go through me first, and Paulie was about ten feet away watching my back in case anyone jumped on me; and I knew that wasn't going to happen. Those pussy boys are as soft as baby shit.

As soon as they were both in the room, Heavy charged at Costello just like he did with me, but Costello didn't have any hands. Just like I expected, he was all mouth. Heavy tossed him around like a rag doll and Costello is not a small guy; probably 5'10", and a 270 pound, sloppy fat, White boy. Heavy swung him around with ease; pinning him in the corner and unleashing three or four of the hardest punches I've ever seen. I'm glad he never got his hands on me. He was a ground and pound type of fighter. With his height and weight, by the second punch, Costello was out cold. I had to run in to stop it before Heavy killed him and caught a murder rap. That shit was over like a Tyson fight in the 90's.

A strange wave of affects happened after the Heavy fight that not even I would have ever predicted. There was another inmate named Don that was half Black and half Spanish. I had showed love to him when he first got on the block. When he was in his seventy-two hour classification process, I hit him with all the things an inmate would need to get started: a cup, bowl, shower shoes, lotion, deodorant, a radio, plus a couple of books and magazines to read. Like I mentioned before, there weren't too many people of color on the block, so I had to look out for my own.

I even told homeboy he could sit at our table when he was out of lockup. When he did get out, everything was cool, but as time passed, even he was getting on my last nerve. He was young; twenty-three…so we were not going to be on the same page as each other on most things. But more than that was the fact that we didn't even really know each other from a hole in the wall before coming into jail, which worsened things. As I have said before, being around someone in such close quarters will make you dislike someone based upon the simplest of things; the way they eat, the way they walk, even their vocabulary and the words they use…every little thing will upset you and that's what was happening with me and Don.

After Paulie and I became cellmates, we started to eat in our cell. Even the sight of Don's eating and the way he spoke made me leave the table that I had been sitting at. He was just getting on my nerves. I would still play a game of spades with him here and there, but it wasn't the same. Since Don was Spanish, and liked speaking it, he became real friendly with one of the Spanish COs – Lucie. I really didn't care for her. Once or twice during my stay at RCDC, sometimes I would wake up and the two of them would be talking at 4:00 in the morning because he ended up working the third shift job more and more. He was getting under my skin, but after the fight with Heavy and Costello, somehow, Lucie found out about it and people started to point the finger at him.

Not really thinking, I mentioned that to his cellmate who couldn't wait to run and start an issue. That, plus the fact that Don had probably began to notice the way I was starting to treat him over the last couple of months, made things change. To him, I was no longer the friendly face that had greeted him when he was locked up for his classification process. So when he heard the info and given the fact that he was already pissed off about getting passed up for the job he was promised and had been given a shitty ground crew maintenance job instead, he had issues with me. The job he was on meant that he had worked the day before in the middle of the summer, weed whacking and other shitty stuff. All of it made his temper short.

Don approached me with a tone in his voice that I didn't necessarily like. The conversation got heated very quickly and we were in each other's faces like to angry pit bulls. We were right on the block in front of everyone. We had seen other White inmates do the same thing before and then back away like punk bitches, cursing and talking shit as they walked away; but we were not about that life. I had even walked away from an argument or two with other inmates before, but for some reason...I'm not sure if it was just the frustration of jail life, or just Don in general...but I couldn't walk away this time.

Without thinking, I shoved him and with 300 to 500 pushups a day, my strength was surprisingly strong. He flew about ten feet backwards; only being held up by a laundry bucket and a flight of stairs. At that point, I knew I had fucked up. I first thought about the job I was about to lose; steak tips, cigs and the rest of it...all out the window. Then I thought about my good time and then I thought about how I could really hurt that kid and the charges that I might get.

This fight was not like the fight I had with Heavy; this one was on the tier in front of everyone: COs, inmates...everyone. When the young kid from New Jersey who was 210 pounds, and six feet tall charged back at me, he brought all of his anger with him. He had been punked and disrespected, and he had to do something about it.

I knew I had fucked up and the only thought I had was to just grab hold of him before it went too far. He came out swinging rights and wildly hooked my head, which I was able to get my left hand up enough to block most of the force of the punch. He still caught my temple though. I still didn't want to lose my cool and hurt the kid, so I went to scoop him up and he continued to swing; catching me slightly with a left and right. I dropped him to the ground and swung him around into one of the cell doors. I was able to ding him with a left hook on his left eye; not hard, but just hard enough to slow him down. Then I put him in a Guillotine choke hold, which is a move that I had put many dudes to sleep with in the past. He wasn't getting out of it.

I could feel his body starting to go limp. When I was surrounded by at least ten COs who were telling me to let him go…I did it quickly; not wanting to get tazed or maced. As I was placing my hands behind my back to get handcuffed, while watching him get handcuffed too, I wondered what I had done. I had just completed six months of good behavior and done the drain with about sixty days left. And in one quick moment, I had jeopardized all that and gave all the White inmates a show. Don and I looked like gorillas: Black inmates fighting in a cage. We were both going back to F Block to be placed on seventy-two hour lockup for fighting and we were definitely getting a D Boarder which is a disciplinary court hearing with the board of COs who decide your fate.

That first twenty-three hours in lockup is always hard for me no matter what the situation is. This time it was really hard because

I had to keep wondering if I was going to lose good time or get more time in the hole. I wouldn't find that out until the D Boarder (Disciplinary hearing). The Corporal came in for me to sign the papers for the hearing and they had more than a week to make the hearing happen. By the time he came in, I had been in the cell for about fourteen hours. My eye had swollen up a bit. But I've suffered worse, so I wasn't worried about it. I have to admit…I did feel ashamed to look at the Corporal that had shown me love since I arrived on February 7th. I felt like a punk.

When you're in the hole, you have nothing but a Bible and maybe a pencil and paper. I would later get a book and some magazines from some inmates that I knew. Those helped ease my mind; I needed it. I had so much on my mind. By the second twenty-three hours, I had knocked out pushups and put ice on my eye that I had gotten from the nurse. I was feeling a little better, but I still had a lot on my mind.

I was able to get word to Don to stick to the statement that it was a mutual combat between us…that way we were both on the same page and neither of us would get a simple assault charge.

Besides, it looks better when going before D Board. Rather than

pointing fingers at each other, Don was cool with it.

By my third day, I was ready to get out of there. I lucked out

though, they placed another inmate in there with me and he was a

solid dude. We talked till later that night to pass the time. He was a

White boy that was serving a year for drugs and he still had five

months left. He had gotten a twenty-four-hour lockup for doing

some dumb shit during yard time, but he was used to it. He had

already had three twenty-four-hour lockups in the last ninety days.

He had been doing time since he was seventeen years old. He had

done a six-year bid in State prison for shooting some one that tried

to rob him. He got two to six years for shooting him and then

another two to six years for shooting at the dude as he ran away,

then another two to six for putting the gun to the guy's partner's

head and forcing him down on his knees and telling him that he

was going to kill him.

Fagen was a gangster ass White boy; the kind that you wouldn't want to rob. The guy that tried to rob him would have gotten away with it; he and his partner told the cops what happened. That was crazy because they were trying to rob him and yet they called the cops because he defended himself.

When Fagen got out of jail, six years later at the age of twenty-four, he spent some time on the outside, but caught a couple smaller bids over the next couple of years. At the age of twenty-eight, he was going to max out his parole and be able to put his youth behind him, but his record would always follow him. The fact that he had spent most of his life in jail meant that he had never really left New England, he had only been to Mass, New Hampshire and Rhode Island for a couple of hours. In a way, I felt bad for him. He was almost thirty years old and had never traveled or experienced anything. He still had time to change his life and do things, but what could he possibly do with a bad record and no life experiences. And it was all because of one mistake at age seventeen. People talk about destiny…but what is his?

We talked until we both fell asleep, and it let me get my mind off my problems for a while, which I was thankful for. After my seventy-two hour lockup, I was happy to get out, but out is an understatement because I was on bottom tier on F Block, which was a big difference from G Block. My tier time was a short one. We were let out from 10:00 am to 2:30 pm, then locked up till the next day. That sucked, but it was still better than the one hour out that I was given during my seventy-two hour lockup.

I also got my property back. What little you have in jail still puts a smile on your face. I got my food back; tuna, oatmeal, soups and other stuff that I needed seeing that I don't eat most of the State food. I was starving. I also got my radio back, books, and most importantly my pad and pen and everything that I had written. My boy Paulie came through like I knew he would. He was my cellmate and he had packed all my shit and added some of his own: a bag of Kool-Aide, some coffee and some food. That was good looking out on his part. He knew on F Block that I wouldn't be eating as good as I did on G Block. He had handled everything with care, packing all my hygiene separate from my books and papers and best of all, nothing was missing.

If your Bunkie doesn't have love for you, things will be missing. We call them cell thieves. They figure you just got lugged, so they won't be seeing you any time soon...maybe never, and who is going to believe an inmate screaming from another block that he is missing soap, soup and books. Actually...who is even going to care? Not the COs for sure. Maybe a few might, but your stuff would be long gone by then. So what Paulie had done was a solid move, but I didn't expect anything less from him. Real recognizes real. I wasn't sure when I was even going to see him again, maybe on my out date if I still have the same one and don't lose my good time. But I wasn't worried I know he will send me a kite when he gets out.

Now I'm on a new block. I know a couple of dudes here, but not many and I can't afford to get in to another fight before my D Board, so I have to keep my head down and my mouth shut. A lot of the dudes here have been on this block for months, so they have backup. I knew a Spanish dude here named Cruz that had just got lugged from G Block and he was a good person to know because he was friendly with everyone and could make things happen for me if I needed him to. The only worries I had was the damn D Board.

Don was on the same block but on a different tier. We had squashed our beef and realized how stupid it was. He had the better part of the day, being let out from 3:30 pm to 10:00 pm. We both are still locked up and waiting for the D Board.

Chapter 8

As I was awaiting the D Boarder, I was placed on bottom tier of F Block. The first couple of days, I had no cellmate, but then I got an odd White guy in my cell. He was to be there for only twenty days for a DWI case. He was in his forties, about 130 pounds soaking wet; not anything that I needed to worry about, but I started to notice that he was a little off.

On the first day, I noticed him talking to himself. I didn't say anything, but by the third day of being locked in the cell with him, I noticed him laughing to himself.

I said, "Well, it's cool if you can smile and laugh in jail."

He simply said, "Oh, I just thought of something."

I waited for him to fill me in, but he never did. Then I noticed him still laughing to himself fifteen minutes later; that started to worry me a bit. Once he climbed on his bunk and continued to do it under his covers, I knew I had to tell someone because if that crazy motherfucker did something to make me kick his ass, at least I would have told somebody.

Later that day, our cell door popped and he was called out to see the mental health doctor. I mentioned what I had seen to the CO. Mind you…this man had turned down his meds two days in a row saying that he only took it as needed. When he returned from seeing the doctor, he finally explained that he had anxiety, depression and some other shit that made him cry out or laugh unexpectedly.

I was glad that he told me because I was really starting to worry about the guy. Shit, if I would have woken up with him standing over me laughing or crying, I would have had to fuck his crazy 130 pound White ass up. It wouldn't have looked good for me to have two fights in one week. I would have never gotten out of this bitch.

I have two days left for them to D board me. I just want it to be over so that I can get on with the rest of the time I have left. I'm down to sixty-seven days and a wake up. Nine weeks more and I'm free. Word on the block is that this White kid named Teddy that left two weeks ago on the ankle bracelet thing is back with a new charge. That fool caught a gun charge. The new ankle bracelet has a microphone on it and his PO overheard him talking about guns. The PO showed up at his house. Now he will serve year plus new charges.

I've heard a lot of crazy things from inmates while doing my bid. My crazy celly started to talk a lot more before he was moved out of my cell. He told me that the reason he was all messed up was because about a year ago, him and his buddy's girlfriend were hanging out. His buddy – her man, was locked up at the time. It was the girl's twenty-first birthday and they were drinking and getting drunk. They decided to go for a ride and since he was already drunk, he let her drive his truck. Well, in his case, just like in mine, drinking and driving don't go well together, and for them it went a lot worse. The girl ended up flipping the car while doing 80 mph. They both were flown to the hospital in Boston on life support. She died, and he was supposed to die, but he lived. He walks with a limp because of the fake hip he has now. He was in a coma for a couple of weeks and his memory will never be the same. He has a brain injury and forgets things a lot.

I knew he was not all there when I had heard him talking and laughing to himself earlier, but I didn't know the half of it. I felt bad for him. For the rest of his life he will be messed up, and he also has to live with the death of that twenty-one year old girl on his plate too. I thought I had a bad birthday, but to die on your twenty-first birthday is crazy. I'm still not sure how to take it. Life is crazy sometimes.

*****

The time for my D Board came and went. The Sergeant that was supposed to hold it didn't show until three days later to even ask questions. When I was done talking, he asked me if Don and I had rehearsed our statements because we both said the same thing. We both said that we were cool, but that we had just had a bad day that day and had since squashed our beef. We both said that we were sorry for our actions.

The Sergeant was cool about it and said that the seventy-two hour lockup was all that would happen. Thank God. I would still get to leave on my out day. Fuck being a gangster, I miss my mama. Real talk.

I stayed on bottom tier for three weeks. Corporal Voight was disappointed in me and I know that was his way to punish me, but I don't blame him. Truth be told, it broke up my bid by putting me around new faces, new stories and a new block.

After the crazy guy left my cell, I got an eighteen-year-old kid that had just started his one-year bid. It was actually a relief to start to see people that were where I was six months ago. The kid only lasted for about a week. He was moved to G Block because he couldn't do cell time, plus he had work release on his paperwork. I caught the kid crying a couple of times. He was young and he really missed his mom, but before he left, he told me his story.

He was drunk and hanging out with some buddies one night. They got him to try to break into a house. He opened the front door and when he heard the alarm sound, he turned around and ran down the street. He was immediately stopped by the police three blocks away from the house. Well, being White and young with nothing stolen, you would think that he would be let go, but no…he had fifty perks in his pocket. He got charged for the drugs and the B&E (breaking and entering) and was sentenced to one year with thirty days pretrial credit and seven months to serve.

Even though he was eighteen, he was about to enter his senior year in high school. Since he was only charged with a misdemeanor his life is not totally over yet; but he won't get his diploma and he will be lucky if he gets his GED. He will miss thanksgiving, Christmas and New Years by being locked here. It will be rough for him, but like they say, Do your own bid. That's what I'm doing.

While I'm on this new block, I've started to play cards with some new people; mostly younger kids in here. I feel bad for them. At their ages, I was taking trips to California, Barbados, Florida and spending money like Donald Trump. A lot of the kids in here are drug addicts. I swear 90% of the people in here are drug addicts. One of the inmates that came in had his butt stuffed with drugs, but he gave them to the wrong people because he was ratted out three days after getting on the block. I knew it would happen. This jail is horrible with that. Someone didn't get what they wanted and the next thing we knew, he was being dragged out of his cell. The block was crazy that night. Tons of people got drug tested and put into the hole. I'm pretty sure the dude that got caught with the drugs will catch new charges. Addicts will do anything to be high.

My next cellmate was also a young addict. He was in jail for stealing checks from his mother. He was not a bad kid, but not a smart one either. At twenty-one, you think you know everything, so whatever you say to them goes in one ear and out the other, so that's basically how I let things go.

The last couple of weeks went by quickly. I have read a lot of books while being locked down for so long. That's all you can really do. I read a couple of James Patterson's books: Alex Cross's Trial, and The Murder of King Tut. I have to give it to Patterson, he has so many books out and he just keeps them coming. I also read, Original Gangster by Frank Lucas, which I thought was good. It was different from the movie, American Gangster. To me, the movie was better. I've always been a big fan of Mobb Deep, so when I got the chance to read the Prodigy autobiography, I thought it was meant to be. I loved his book! There was so much I didn't know about him that he spoke about in the book. It was nice to get to know more about him seeing as though I grew up on his music; especially the second tape, The Infamous Mobb Deep, which I think was a classic. That tape almost got me in so much trouble over the years. I thought that was the hardest out bumping. That shit…"An Eye for an Eye" will always be one of my favorite songs of all time.

Prodigy has a quote in the book that he says. It is the most important info of the book and I like how it flowed. He says, "Yesterday is gone and tomorrow doesn't count unless you take care of your priorities right now." Prodigy was deep and true.

I also read a book by Neil Gaiman, American Gods, which now lets me know where the saying comes from of, Don't judge a book by its cover. It has a tree on the cover. I would have never even opened the book if another inmate hadn't explained it to me. I'm glad I did thought. I like the idea of the book and his style of writing.

Now, another book that people tried to get me to read while I was in jail caught me off guard. It was the Hunger Games. When the movie came out, I wasn't in jail and I remember seeing previews of two White people running around in the desert. I remember thinking, Hungry White people running around...well, I'll show you some hungry Blacks in the projects running around! I come from a time when food stamps were paper and came in a booklet and crack was ruining families. Now THEY were hungry. There was no way I was going to see that movie or read the book. Shit...what could it show me? No crack and no food stamps? HA! But like anyone that doesn't have an open mind, I was wrong. I read the first book and searched for the second and third like it was crack. They are books that you don't want to put down and the whole idea of the plot is very interesting. I'm sure in the future I will find out more about things before I just push them away. You have to be open minded with everything you do in life.

Which brings me to my next quote that caught my eye. It was not in a book, but in an article. Pharrell, the rapper, said, "Just like that, the moments gone and the moments ahead of that, you can't see. We remember the past, but we can't go back and we can't touch the future, so we are trapped in the present." Pharrell is deep and real.

My time in jail has given me a different outlook on a lot of things, and life is one of them. Two people that I have done time with over the last seven months left jail and died. The first was an inmate named Hanson. Not to talk bad about the dead, but I never really liked him much. There were so many stories about him; from raping his brother and his brother committing suicide because of it, to other stories. He had this look in his eyes that is hard to explain, but he was not right for sure. He had just spent twenty-four months in jail when he got out, and he didn't even last forty-eight hours on the outside. He overdosed and whoever was with him dumped his body behind a Walmart. That's a sucky ass way to go out.

Next was a guy named Oberg. Now, Oberg was a cool guy. I actually sat with him at breakfast for a couple of months before he was released. He had this saying which he always said in the morning, "One more day closer to a big fat plate of cocaine." After saying that he would look at his arm and say, "You better get ready to party!" He also overdosed once he was out. I guess it was not a surprise with all the things he said while in the joint. I guess I still didn't expect it. He had a younger daughter. What a shame.

A lot of addicts that leave here have worries about things like that because they know that they have problems and jail is the only place that they are clean. They know that when they hit the streets, they will hit the drugs again. That's like the saying that I've said before, They didn't get arrested, they got rescued. Me, on the other hand, I worry about being broke and what will I do when I get out. Will I pimp? Will I sell drugs? I'd like to say no, but just like an addict, I'm addicted to money and the lifestyle.

My time is getting closer for me to be able to walk out these doors. My boy Paulie V. walks out in a day. I leave thirty-two days after him. I'm worried about Paulie V. He was...or is addicted and he is going to have a lot of temptation once he gets out. I wish him the best and hope he stays strong. I'll be right by his side when I get out...trying to keep the needle out of his hand, but he has thirty-two days to fuck up, so it's all in God's hands with him. We will just have to wait and see what happens.

Chapter 9

It's hard to sleep when you are not dreaming right. The whole thing with Raquel and the house is bothering me. A couple of weeks ago, out of the blue, she contacted my mother trying to convince her to talk to me so that I'd just sign off on the house. I've been trying to fight it from jail and the Court has been giving me more time, but I'm not sure how it will play out because the jail has messed up some of my legal mail that has to do with the house.

Raquel hit my mother with a sob story about her getting a tumor removed and her health issues. I'm sure it was all blown out of proportion a bit. My mother explained that I was upset because she lied on the paperwork stating that I never put any money toward the house, which was the biggest of the lies. Raquel said she did it not because she wanted to fight with me, but because she was worrying about her health issues. I did not understand her thought process behind that. She's a smart girl...better yet, a smart woman. She knows that the whole time of us owning the house that I was in drug dealer state of mind and paid for everything in cash. The receipts that I did keep, I gave to her years ago for her to use to file her taxes.

She is smart. She knows it will be hard for me to prove to the courts that I'm easily $40,000 into the house. I taught her well; like they say, Don't hate the playa hate the game. She went as far as contacting my older female cousin that she has always had a bond with, and asked her to write me in jail and get me to sign off on the house. My cousin is no fool either. She contacted my mother and explained what was going on, knowing damn well I would have laughed in her face if she would have tried that stupid shit with me.

My mother is no fool either; shit...she raised a thoroughbred hustler. She simply told Raquel that she would pray for her and will speak to me. When she did speak to me she said the same thing I said, "This bitch is out of her mind!"

Gotta love my mom. She is crazy!

I've even gone as far as trying to get my mom to text Raquel and tell her that I would have signed the papers if she hadn't lied. I was trying to get her to admit it over a text message so that I would have some kind of proof, but deep down inside, I knew Raquel was too smart for that shit.

She simply said, "Don't worry about it. We will handle it when he gets out."

*****

I'm not sure what my dream last night meant. All I know is that Raquel got over on me in it and I hate to lose...even in my dreams. All I can do is see how it all plays out. The closer I get to leaving this place, the harder it gets to deal with. You would think that after spending a year in here, that the last thirty days would be easier, but you would be wrong. It's worse. At this point, all I can think of is freedom. I've heard people say you only do two days...the day you walk in and the day you leave. I'm not sure who came up with that dumb ass shit, because I know damn well that I've done every day in this motherfuckin' place.

A lot of things have happened over the last couple of months on F Block. First of all, I was reading the paper and the dude I worked with on the third shift floors when I first got here was in the paper. He had gotten arrested for driving with no license and possession of heroin. He left here on May 23rd. I'm surprised he lasted as long as he did...almost two and a half months. He is stupid. He had a seven and a half to fifteen hanging over his head. All he had to do was stay clean for a year or so on parole, but I guess when you are an addict, that's easier said than done.

The second thing that happened was that last week a White boy got knocked out and shit on himself. I've heard of dudes pissing on themselves, but never shitting on themselves. I guess that's where the saying, He got the shit kicked out of him came from.

I also got a package from Heavy last night. He leaves in a few days. The package was full with commissary items. That was good looking out on his behalf. I'll definitely get up with him on the streets and see how he is living.

Like I said before, sometimes in jail you hear some of the craziest stories of how people ended up here. The one that a White boy named Daily told me is one of them. He had just spent six months in here for a crime he didn't commit. I know what you are thinking...all convicts say they are innocent, but this is different. He explained to me that he and his buddy were drinking and had just missed the last call at the bar and his boy was going on and on about how he would do anything for another drink.

So, without thinking that he had it in him, he told his buddy, "Well, go down to the corner store and just kick in the window and take the beer. I'll be here waiting."

His buddy said, "Fuck it, I will."

Daily thought that by the time his boy got to the corner store, he would have come to his senses, but Daily was wrong. The dude came back with a thirty rack. They drank and laughed about it. Well, what Daily didn't know was that his stupid buddy also stole scratch off lottery tickets and was arrested the next day trying to cash them in. When he was arrested he told the police that daily told him to break into the store, so the police came and arrested Daily for conspiracy to commit burglary. He was shocked. With no bail money and a public pretender...I mean, public defender, he was sentenced to twelve months; six months suspended, but six months to mandatorily serve. It's crazy how things happen. Daily's buddy got four months, but only served ninety days with good time.

Sometimes I'm not sure if justice is justice, but who am I to say anything. I got locked up for a year on my first violation, when I've seen White kids walk in and out of this jail on numerous violations and they only serve seven to fourteen days. There was a kid that they called Red that just left on his seventh violation. I've seen him twice in the last month. Red told me that the judge told him that on his next violation, he will get a year. His next one? Yeah, where is the justice in that?

COs

September 12, 2013

I haven't given much time in this book to talk about COs (Correctional Officers). Those guys or females are a rare breed and not in a good way. Well, you have some of them that come to work just to collect a check and they don't let the power go to their heads. But there are a few that take the power surge to a whole new level. I think that most of them were either picked on in high school or have other mental issues. I can't tell you what those other mental issues are, but I'd really like to know.

Today a CO named Norton entered the cell to take a pair of pants out the window that were blocking the sun from coming in. Most COs don't care about stuff like that, but I'm not sure why Norton is such a dick, but he is. Maybe it is because his wife is a Corporal here and he does not have any rank. Or maybe there is some other issue that I haven't been able to figure out, but he is a dick none the less. He is also the one that took extra pillows that me and my Bunkie had. Mind you…I've had those pillows for over a month and no other CO has taken them. I know that as an inmate we are only supposed to have one, so I understand the rules, but it was the look on his face when he left the cell with them that was crazy. He acted like he had just hit the Lotto. Now if that's the highlight of our day, there's a problem. Hopefully he will never lose his job because when he has to fill out another job application, under skills he will have to put that he has a keen eye for taking extra pillows, blankets and mats from inmates, and that he has mastered the art of being a dick while he does it.

Then you have another CO named Zapa. That kid is a piece of work. He is only twenty-two years old and has to be one of the biggest dickheads that worked at the rock (RCDC). Now he really had to be picked on in high school. He lets the little power he has go to his head. It's to the point that I'm sure 90% of the inmates would love to smack the shit out of him, but that's a three to seven charge, and the inmates know that and so does he. Karma is a bitch. Someone will see him on the streets. Neither one of those COs would make it at a State prison where motherfuckers are serving life or are in there for murder, but in a county jail, that shit can slide.

I could go on about those COs for days, but I really can't give them that type of time.

Females

Another subject that's been on my mind for the last seven months is one that is major for me during my bid, but I try my hardest not to think about it. Sometimes it's impossible. It's females. I miss everything about them; their smell, hair, lips, hips, butt, tits, pussy, feet, thighs, eyes, touch…everything that a woman has to offer. At this point, I even miss their bitchiness. I always took them for granted because they came to me so easy, but now I'd do anything for just some affection.

After being surrounded by men for over seven months, even the female COs and nurses that I wouldn't normally have spit on 220 days ago, I'd wife up now. You can smell their perfume from ten feet away. Jail smells like ass, corn chips, body odor and sweaty balls. So when something nice like the smell of a female's perfume crosses your path, you are sure to appreciate it. It's the little things in life that are so big in jail. I can't wait to be touched by a female again. I will sit back and take it all in with a smile on my face. Females are another subject that I could go on forever about, but I'm going to take it easy.

Chapter 10

I'm down to twenty-four days and I'll be free. When you are this close to getting out, it's like every day drags on forever. It's also like the world is on your shoulders. Truth be told, I can't wait to be free. Some of these dudes that are locked up do their time without thinking about freedom until the last moment. I've thought about freedom my whole bid and it won't hit me until I'm driving away from this place for good.

The clock is ticking down. Twenty-four days. Three weeks and three days. A little over 576 hours. The time can't go quick enough for me. I'm ready. I have a lot of ideas of what I want to do and accomplish. I know if I put my mind to it, I can do anything, so I will be leaving this place with a positive outlook; that's for sure.

*****

Time is going by quick. I am seven days out from being free. I've been working out like crazy; pushups, jumping jacks, and shadow boxing. I've also been playing cards and reading books. I've noticed in jail that there is a lot of talk about classic movies and the lines that are in those movies. There is also a lot of talk about classic songs. You can go on for hours trying to one up another person with that type of knowledge. It definitely passes the time and gives you thoughts of when times were better and sitting on a couch watching a classic like The Golden Child with Eddie Murphy or riding in a car bumping 2Pac or Biggie.

Most of my time here has been spent reading books. I read another James Patterson book, Tick Tock, which I liked. It was different from the other two books of his that I read. I like his style. I also picked up a book by Tim Allen, the comedian from Home Improvement. He sparked my interest because I knew he had spent time in prison for selling drugs and that's where he started his comedy career. The book was called, Don't Stand too Close to a Naked Man. I complete every book that I start, but I just couldn't keep reading his book. It lost my attention right around 110 pages into it. I did get one good quote out of those 100 or so pages.

Tim said, "Anyone who says prison is great or they can do it – fine…so explain to me why if you open the door, everyone would walk away."

He was so right with that statement. So many people in this jail try to act tough an say they do their time and this ain't shit, but all I know is I want to go home. I wanted to go home since day one. It is not cool to be in jail.

One of the best books I think that I have read since I got here has been Mafia Dynasty by John H. Davis. Now that book came to me at a perfect time toward the end of my bid. When you are anxious and thinking about the streets, it helps to have something to free your mind. Not to mention, I love any book that goes into depth about the mafia; especially my man, John Gottie, aka the

Dapper Don, aka the Teflon Don. Mafia Dynasty talks about the rise and fall of the mafia and a lot of important people in it, like Lucky Luciano, Frank Costello, Meyer Lansky, Vito Genovese, Albert Anastasia, Carlo Gambino, Paul Castellano and Sammy the Bull. There were so many quotes that I got from that book that touched me in different ways and reminded me of my life and the things I had done in it.

Furberia is an Italian word that means, a wary cleverness, slyness, an astuteness of one who figures out all the angles before he makes a move. More than anything, I need Furberia. When I leave this place, I need to be on point. I've been really thinking of tattooing it on my left wrist to go with Seize the Day and Seize the moment which I already have tattooed on me to remind me to do just that.

Paul Castellano was taped by the Feds talking about his philosophy of life in the mob and I think his philosophy is so right about hustling and just the street life in general.

He said, "This life of ours…this wonderful life…if you can get through life like this and get away with it…hey, that's great. But it's very, very unpredictable. There's so many ways you can screw it up. So you gotta think. Ya gotta be patient A lot of guys…their yanking their zipper before their dick is put away and they don't know when to zip their fucking mouths shut either. I tell em, 'You listen, you learn. You talk, you teach."

That is so true if you have ever lived the street life, I know you're thinking the same damn thing. Now, on the other hand, when things are bad, they are bad. Like Joe N. Gallo, a mob boss, tries to philosophy, "I mean…you spend your life working on this thing. This thing of ours…you think you are doing right, and then something happens. Something goes off track. You get old. It doesn't look as good as it used to look. Disappointed. You end up disappointed, and the bitch of it is you can't put your finger on what went wrong. You're doing good. You're doing good. You're doing good…now somehow, the way it all ends up…you ain't done shit. It all ends up small. It all ends up sour." Joe's Fed tapes…now that's the way I also feel at times.

Castellano's thought are how I felt at age thirteen to twenty – five, and Gallos' thoughts are mine from age twenty-five to thirty-five. It's strange how things happen and how life throws you curve balls, but you must keep your head up and keep it moving.

At the end of the day, I have to agree with my man John Gotti for my final thoughts, "I know what's going on…I'm in the fuckin' hunt. Me…I'll always be alright." That is from John Gotti's Fed tapes.

Chapter 11

The last week went by quickly. It's 10:00 o'clock on October 7, 2013. I'm down to my last nine hours. I'm so ready for the streets. I passed the time this last week by working out and playing cards. I also read another book; 441 pages long. I read it in a couple of days. It was called, The Hot House, by Pete Earley. It was about Leavenworth Prison. I really liked how the book was written. It talked about prison life and a lot of different inmates and staff that were there during the time period. It talked about one person for a chapter and then another the next chapter; intertwining all of them over the course of the book.

With all of the books that I've read, I've noticed that there are so many different styles of writing. I have so much to learn if I want to continue to write. Like I said, before, I'm not sure what I am going to do when I get out of here. I'm not sure if I am going to be good or bad. I heard another quote recently that I like. I'm not sure who wrote it, but I like it.

"If you're worried, you're living in the future. If you have regrets, you're living in the past. If you're content, you're living in the moment."

Well, I'm not worried. I don't have any regrets. I'm not content. But what I do know is…whatever happens with the rest of my life after I walk out of these jail doors, it's all in god's hands.

To be continued…

~by Tarik Adams, AKA Mr. Handle Ur Biz

To be continued…